The MAILBOX®

The Education Center®

MATH
INDEPENDENT
PRACTICE SUPER SIMPLE!

grades 4-6

 **144** EASY-TO-USE IDEAS FOR SKILL REINFORCEMENT

- ☑ Addition & subtraction
- ☑ Multiplication & division
- ☑ Measurement
- ☑ Geometry
- ☑ Algebra
- ☑ Fractions
- ☑ Decimals
- ☑ **AND LOTS MORE!**

ENOUGH FOR
4 activities for every week
OF THE SCHOOL YEAR

Managing Editor: Peggy Hambright

Editorial Team: Becky S. Andrews, Diane Badden, Amber Barbee, Amy Barsanti, Brooke Beverly, Kimberley Bruck, Karen A. Brudnak, Kitty Campbell, Pam Crane, Chris Curry, Colleen Dabney, Mary Davis, Dee Demyan, Lynette Dickerson, Ann Fisher, Sarah Foreman, Theresa Lewis Goode, Tazmen Hansen, Terry Healy, Marsha Heim, Lori Z. Henry, John Hughes, Debra Liverman, Dorothy C. McKinney, Thad H. McLaurin, Lisa Mellon, Shawna Miller, Sharon Murphy, Jennifer Nunn, Jennifer Otter, Amy Payne, Gail Peckumn, Kristin Priola, Mark Rainey, Greg D. Rieves, Hope Rodgers, Eliseo De Jesus Santos II, Rebecca Saunders, Marsha Schmus, Renee S_____ Thomas, Suzette Westhoff, Zane Williard

www.themailbox.com

D1310390

©2008 The Mailbox® Books
All rights reserved.
ISBN10 #1-56234-848-5 • ISBN13 #978-1-56234-848-9

Printed in the United States
10 9 8 7 6 5 4 3 2

HPS 227863

Table of Contents

To use the table of contents as a checklist, make a copy of pages 2 and 3. Staple or clip each copy on top of its original page. Each time you use an activity, check its box. Start each school year with fresh copies of the pages.

Skills Index on pages 111-112.

Roll and Write!

Place value

Materials:
student copies of the recording sheet on page 76
die

A student rolls the die and writes on the recording sheet the number he rolled. Next, he writes a multi-digit number using the number he rolled to represent the specified place value. He identifies the rolled digit by drawing a box around it. Then he repeats the steps to complete the page.

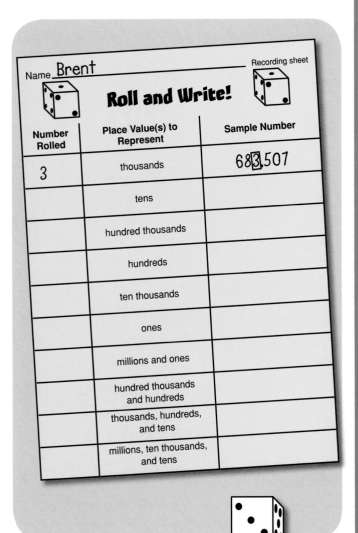

Ten Cups

Place value

Materials:
copy of the number clues on page 76
10 disposable cups labeled from 0 through 9
decimal point cutout
2 comma cutouts
envelope containing the answer (shown below)

A student follows the clues and moves the cups and punctuation cutouts around as needed to build the mystery number. When she's finished, she checks her solution by looking in the envelope.

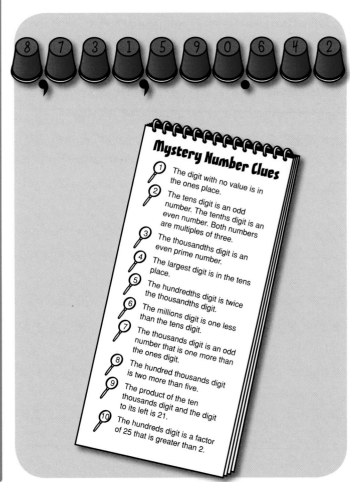

Showtime

Elapsed time

Materials:
movie listing from a newspaper
6 index cards labeled as shown
paper

A student selects a movie from the listing and copies its title and start times on her paper. She circles one start time. She also chooses an index card and lists the time shown on it as the "current time." Then she determines the amount of time she must wait until the circled showing and writes it on her paper. She repeats the steps, choosing a different movie and time card until all the time cards have been used.

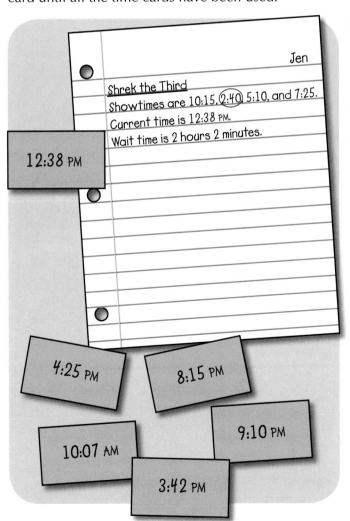

Dream Machine

Polygons

Materials:
pattern blocks or templates of various polygons
paper
colored pencils or markers

A student designs a futuristic machine by tracing polygon shapes on paper. He colors the tracings and gives his machine a name that hints at its use. He also lists each polygon he used to create his magnificent machine.

Heads-or-Tails Math

Basic facts

Materials:
flash cards
2 index cards labeled as shown
coin
paper

A student shuffles the flash cards, divides them into two piles (answers facedown), and places a labeled card in front of each pile. Next, she tosses the coin and draws a flash card from the corresponding pile (heads or tails). She says the answer and flips the card over to check. If her answer is correct, she awards herself the appropriate points (Heads = 2 points, Tails = 1 point). After she draws all the flash cards, she totals her score. She repeats the activity as time allows, trying to improve her score with each additional round.

A Trio of Categories

Decimals

Materials:
copy of the number cards on page 77, cut apart
poster board with a 3-circle Venn diagram labeled as shown

A student sorts the number cards into groups according to the diagram's headings. Then he arranges the cards in the diagram until he has correctly placed three cards in each region.

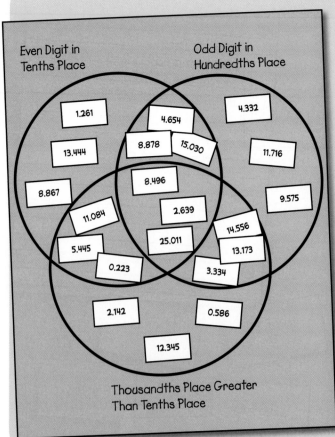

Find Five Pairs

Perimeter

Materials:
copy of the cards on page 78, cut apart and
   mounted on separate index cards
paper

A student finds the perimeter of the shape on each
card and records the measurements on his paper.
Then he determines the shapes that have matching
perimeters and lists that information.

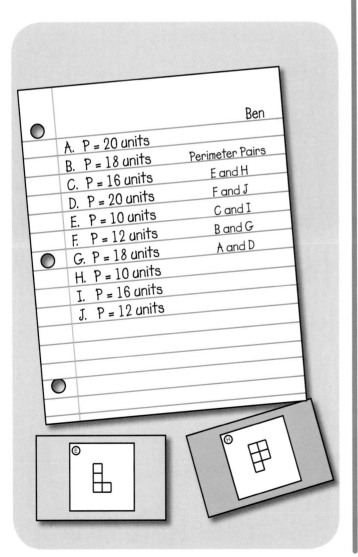

Ben

A. P = 20 units
B. P = 18 units   Perimeter Pairs
C. P = 16 units
D. P = 20 units   E and H
E. P = 10 units   F and J
F. P = 12 units   C and I
G. P = 18 units   B and G
H. P = 10 units   A and D
I. P = 16 units
J. P = 12 units

Calories Count!

Bar graph

Materials:
copy of the calorie chart from page 79
paper
ruler
colored pencils or crayons

A student uses the data in the chart to make a bar
graph comparing the calories in five or more different
sandwiches. He colors the graph and then summarizes the results.

Sandwich Shack

Sandwich	Calories	Sandwich	Calories
Bossy Aussie	260	Gold Rigger	560
Burrito Bandito	490	Ham Slammer	530
Cheddar Shredder	420	Happy Pappy	330
Crusty Musty	270	Shopper Stopper	530
Feast Beast	870	Snack Stack	550
Fish Squisher	730	Sourdough Sloppy Joe	640

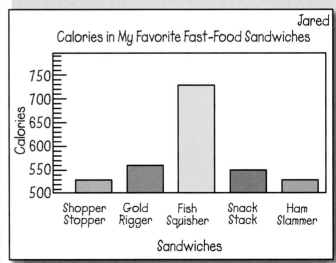

Jared

Calories in My Favorite Fast-Food Sandwiches

"Eggs-act" Comparisons

Comparing whole numbers

Materials:
bag of dried beans
sanitized egg carton with its inside lid labeled as shown
list of paired numbers
paper

A student places the appropriate number of beans in each egg-carton cup to represent the digits of the first pair of numbers, using a separate row for each number. Then she compares the number in the top row to the number in the bottom row and records the comparison on her paper. She repeats the steps to compare each remaining number pair on the list.

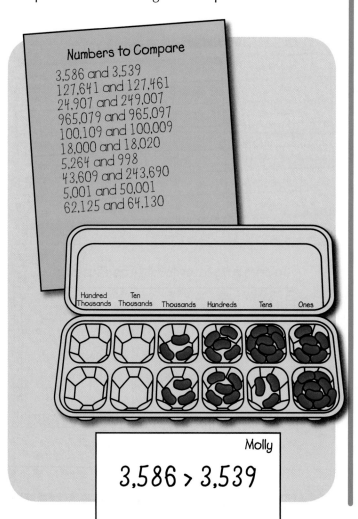

Numbers to Compare

3,586 and 3,539
127,641 and 127,461
24,907 and 249,007
965,079 and 965,097
100,109 and 100,009
18,000 and 18,020
5,264 and 998
43,609 and 243,690
5,001 and 50,001
62,125 and 64,130

| Hundred Thousands | Ten Thousands | Thousands | Hundreds | Tens | Ones |

Molly

3,586 > 3,539

Roll 'em!

Comparing decimals

Materials:
2 dice
paper

A student rolls the dice and writes a decimal on his paper using the numbers rolled. He rolls the dice again to form and record a second decimal. Then he writes the appropriate symbol between the decimals to compare them. He repeats the steps until he has compared ten pairs of decimals.

0.63 > 0.54

Craig

Shoebox Surprises

Linear measurement

Materials:
student copies of the recording sheet on page 80
shoebox filled with 10 items
ruler

A student removes an item from the box and records the item's name on the recording sheet. She measures the item according to each specified unit, records her measurements, and then returns the item to the box. She continues in this manner until she has measured each item in the box.

Extend It!

Patterning

Materials:
paper strip programmed with a numerical pattern starter
paper strip labeled with a geometric pattern starter
paper
markers

A student takes a programmed strip and copies the pattern starter on his paper. He identifies and extends the pattern. He also gives an explanation. Then he repeats the steps with the remaining strip.

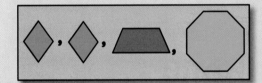

6.5, 6.9, 6.7, 7.1, 6.9...

Connor

6.5, 6.9, 6.7, 7.1, 6.9, 7.3, 7.1, 7.5, 7.3, 7.7, 7.5...

The pattern is adding four tenths and then subtracting two tenths.

The pattern is blue rhombus, blue rhombus, red trapezoid, and green octagon.

Dial Up

Ordering whole numbers

Materials:
phone book
4 paper strips labeled as shown
paper

A student selects a paper strip. In the book, she finds the phone number of someone whose last name starts with the first letter listed on the strip. She copies the phone number as a seven-digit number on her paper. Then she finds and copies the phone number of a person whose last name begins with the second letter listed on the strip. This number must be greater than or less than the first phone number to match the directions on her strip. She continues in this manner until she has listed four numbers in the order directed. Then she repeats the steps with each remaining strip.

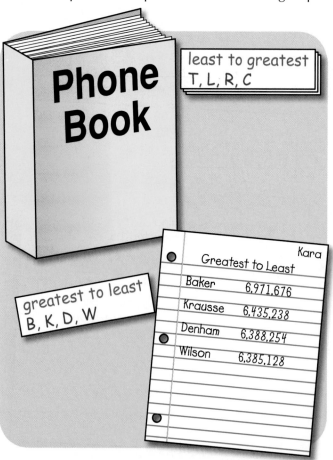

least to greatest
T, L, R, C

Phone Book

greatest to least
B, K, D, W

Kara

Greatest to Least

Baker	6,971,676
Krausse	6,435,238
Denham	6,388,254
Wilson	6,385,128

Dream Teams

Ordering decimals

Materials:
student copies of the batting averages chart on page 79
2 markers
paper

A student uses a marker to highlight any nine names on his chart. He copies the players' names and corresponding batting averages on his paper, writing them in order from greatest to least. Then he repeats the steps using the other marker.

Team Roster

👆 Player ⚾	Batting Average
Tank Aaron	0.333
Mickey Bantle	0.313
Frank Bromas	0.285
Tom Clavine	0.188
Wade Cloggs	0.289
Cal Dipken	0.304
Ken Driffey	0.303
Reggie Gackson	0.312
Mike Jiazza	0.297
Joe Kli	0.299
Derek	0.2??
Orel M	
Rand	
Gre	
Will	
Alb	
Sa	
R	
D	

Michael

Red Team		Blue Team	
Tank Aaron	0.333	Albert Nujols	0.311
Mickey Bantle	0.313	Sammy Rosa	0.310
Reggie Gackson	0.312	Andruw Zones	0.306
Cal Dipken	0.304	Willie Nays	0.300
Ken Driffey	0.303	Joe Klizaggio	0.299
Chipper Vones	0.302	Derek Leter	0.298
Greg Naddux	0.215	Mike Jiazza	0.297
Randy Mohnson	0.205	Wade Cloggs	0.289
Orel Mershiser	0.197	Tom Clavine	0.188

The Clock Is Ticking!

Elapsed time

Materials:
paper strip labeled as shown
index cards labeled with different times
paper

A student reads the problem on the paper strip. Then he takes two cards and solves the problem using the times on the cards. He also explains on his paper how he got his answer. He repeats the steps until he has solved the problem three times, using different cards each time.

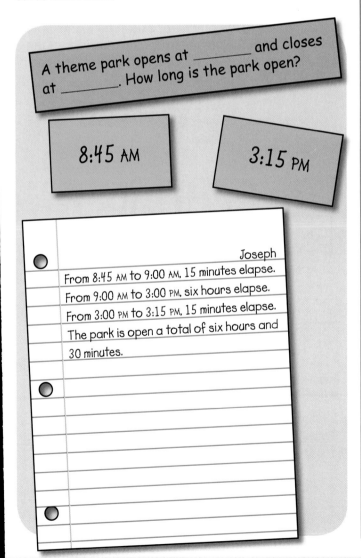

A theme park opens at _____ and closes at _____. How long is the park open?

8:45 AM

3:15 PM

Joseph

From 8:45 AM to 9:00 AM, 15 minutes elapse.
From 9:00 AM to 3:00 PM, six hours elapse.
From 3:00 PM to 3:15 PM, 15 minutes elapse.
The park is open a total of six hours and 30 minutes.

Fishing for Shapes

Similar and congruent shapes

For partners

Materials:
copy of the cards on page 81 for each player
scissors
crayons or markers

Each student cuts her cards apart and writes her name on the back of each one. One child combines and shuffles the cards, deals each player seven cards, and stacks the remaining cards facedown. The students then play the game according to the rules of Go Fish, using the terms *similar* and *congruent* to ask for cards.

Check, Please!

Money

Materials:
student copies of the guest check on
    page 82, cut apart
2 take-out menus
calculator
play money

Each student selects a menu and lists three or more items and their prices on a guest check. He calculates the total cost and uses play money to "pay" his partner for the bill. His partner takes the payment and then gives him back the appropriate change. The pair continues in this manner as time allows.

Guest Check

Date	Table Number	Number in Party	Check Number
hamburger		$2	25
french fries		$1	50
milk shake		$2	75
Total		$6	50

> Here's three dollars and fifty cents in change.

Fill the Cartons!

Equivalent decimals

Materials:
student copies of page 83
scissors
tape
paper

A student cuts out the egg cartons and cuts the cards apart. She sets the egg carton cutouts aside and sorts the cards into three groups: two sets of six equivalent decimals and one set of 12 unrelated decimals. She tapes one set of equivalent decimal cards to the sections of one egg carton half and those for the second set to the other egg carton half. She tapes the 12 unrelated decimal cards to the sections of the whole carton. She then lists the three different sets of numbers on her paper.

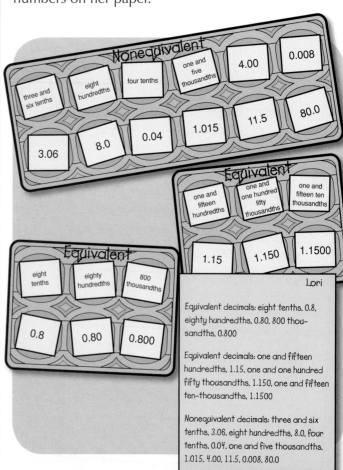

Nonequivalent

| three and six tenths | eight hundredths | four tenths | one and five thousandths | 4.00 | 0.008 |
| 3.06 | 8.0 | 0.04 | 1.015 | 11.5 | 80.0 |

Equivalent

| one and fifteen hundredths | one and one hundred fifty thousandths | one and fifteen ten thousandths |
| 1.15 | 1.150 | 1.1500 |

Equivalent

| eight tenths | eighty hundredths | 800 thousandths |
| 0.8 | 0.80 | 0.800 |

Lori

Equivalent decimals: eight tenths, 0.8, eighty hundredths, 0.80, 800 thousandths, 0.800

Equivalent decimals: one and fifteen hundredths, 1.15, one and one hundred fifty thousandths, 1.150, one and fifteen ten-thousandths, 1.1500

Nonequivalent decimals: three and six tenths, 3.06, eight hundredths, 8.0, four tenths, 0.04, one and five thousandths, 1.015, 4.00, 11.5, 0.008, 80.0

Guess, Fill, and Measure

Capacity

Materials:
3 sanitized containers with labels removed, labeled 1–3
liquid measuring cup
paper

Possible container combinations include a plastic soda bottle, a salad dressing bottle, and a margarine tub.

A student studies the size and shape of each container and guesses which will hold the greatest and least amount of water. She records her guesses on her paper. She also draws on her paper a chart like the one shown. Next, she fills each container with water, measures the amount it holds, and records the capacity in the chart. Then she writes a statement about the results.

Natalie

I think container 3 will hold the most water and container 2 will hold the least water.

Container Number	Amount of Water It Holds
1	
2	
3	

What's the Chance?

Probability

Materials:
3 small paper bags, each labeled with a different question and answer
small items for each bag
paper

Possible items for a bag include paper squares, buttons, or pattern blocks.

A student reads the question on one bag and uses the bag's contents to help her answer the question. She writes an answer on her paper and then looks at the bottom of the bag to check her answer. She repeats the steps until she has answered the question on each bag.

Bag One
What is the probability of drawing from this bag a paper square that is not red?

5 out of 6, or $\frac{5}{6}$

Set 6

Luck of the Roll

Addition

Materials:
4 copies of the number cards on page 84, cut apart
die
paper

A student shuffles the cards and stacks them face-down. Next, she rolls the die to determine the number of digits in her first number. She draws that number of cards, arranges them to form a number, and records the resulting number on her paper. She repeats the steps a second time to form another number or multiple times to form a column of numbers. Then she finds the sum.

Go With the Flow!

Decimals

Materials:
copy of the decimal cards on page 85,
    cut apart and folded with the text
    to the outside and the edges taped
student copies of the recording sheet on page 85

A student shuffles the cards and arranges them in a row with the starting numbers faceup. He records the mixed decimal from each successive card in the appropriate box of his recording sheet. He follows the directions to complete each column. Then he turns the cards over to check his answers.

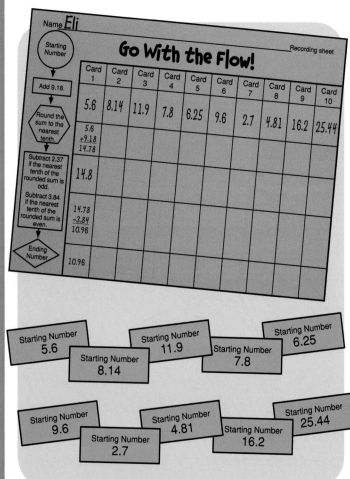

Ant Farms

Perimeter

Materials:
6 index cards labeled as shown
paper
ruler
green crayon

A student draws an ant in the left corner of her paper. To draw her first farm, she chooses one length card and one width card. She draws a rectangle with measurements equal to those on the cards she selected and labels the sides accordingly. Then she finds the farm's perimeter and records the measurement in the rectangle. She repeats the steps, using a different pair of cards each time, until she finds the perimeter of three different farms. She then outlines in green the farm with the greatest perimeter.

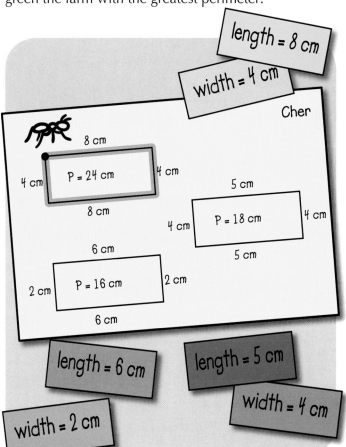

True or False?

Variables

Materials:
copy of the cards on page 86, cut apart

A student turns the answer key card facedown. Next, he reads the cards and sorts them into two piles: true and false. Then he checks his work with the key.

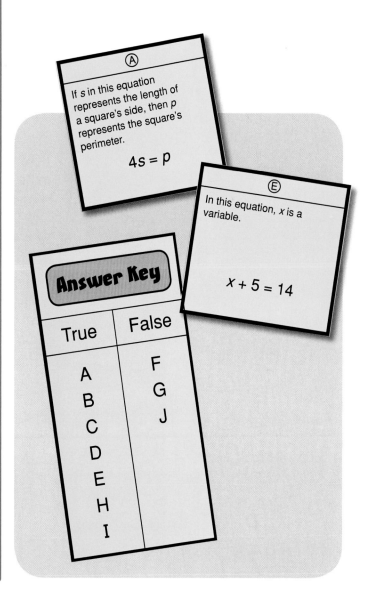

Closer to Zero

Subtraction

Materials:
2 paper bags, each containing a set of number cards from page 84
paper

For partners

Each student takes a bag, draws four cards from his bag, and arranges the cards to form two numbers whose difference is close to zero. Each partner then writes his numbers as a subtraction problem on his paper. The students solve the problems and the child with the smaller difference circles his answer. The partners return the cards to the bag and repeat the steps as time allows, each time taking two more cards from the bag than before. The partner with more circled answers at the end wins.

Water Data Disks

Problem solving

Materials:
4 paper circles, each labeled with a different numerical fact shown below
paper

A student uses the data on the circles to write three or more word problems on her paper. Then she solves the problems.

About $\frac{2}{3}$ of Earth's surface is water.

About 97% of Earth's water is seawater. 2% is frozen in glaciers and ice, and 1% is fresh water.

About 74% of the water used at home is used in the bathroom.

A washing machine uses about 50 gallons of water for each load.

Tazmen

1. About how much of Earth's surface is not water?

$$1 = \frac{3}{3}$$
$$\frac{\frac{2}{3} = \frac{2}{3}}{\frac{1}{3}}$$

2. What fraction of Earth's water is fresh water?

$$1\% = \frac{1}{100}$$

3. What percent of the water used at home is not used in the bathroom?

$$\frac{\begin{array}{r} 100\% \\ -74\% \end{array}}{26\%}$$

4. If my mom does a half load of wash, how much water will she use?

25 gallons
$$2\overline{)50}$$
$$\underline{-4}$$
$$10$$
$$\underline{-10}$$
$$0$$

What Should I Wear?

Temperature

Materials:
2 paper bags labeled as shown
8 paper strips labeled as shown
drawing paper
crayons

A student divides his paper into four sections and then selects two strips from each bag. He writes the temperature from each strip in a different section of his paper. Then, in each section, he illustrates a scene in which he shows himself dressed in an outfit he would wear if the weather were that temperature.

Around Town

Line segments

Materials:
paper
crayons

A student draws on half of her paper a map of a town that includes parallel, perpendicular, and intersecting streets. On the other half of her paper, she writes about the streets' relationships.

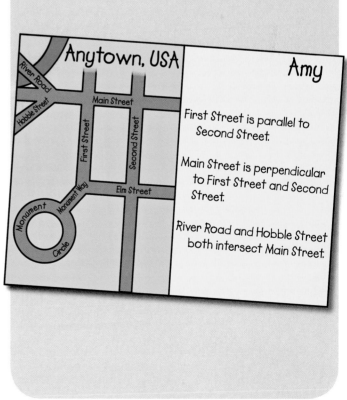

Make 'em Grow!

Estimation

Materials:
index card labeled with a designated place value
paper

A student draws boxes on his paper as shown. He writes an addition problem in the first box, rounds each addend to the designated place in the adjacent box, and then finds the estimated sum. He repeats the activity four times, each time writing a problem that adds another place value, creating a larger estimated sum than the previous one. When he's finished, he repeats the steps using subtraction problems.

Addition		Subtraction	
2.18 +5.63	2.2 +5.6 7.8	7.56 −2.34	7.6 −2.3 5.3
13.14 +36.39	13.1 +36.4 49.5	39.01 −16.67	39.0 −16.7 22.3
545.08 +268.14	545.1 +268.1 813.2	418.68 −396.07	418.7 −396.1 22.6
6,493.45 +2,018.16	6,493.5 +2,018.2 8,511.7	1,476.05 −1,218.67	1,476.1 −1,218.7 257.4
12,411.89 +10,650.42	12,411.9 +10,650.4 23,062.3	29,698.53 −26,004.76	29,698.5 −26,004.8 3,693.7
		Stephen	

tenths place

Over the Top

Multiples of 10

Materials:
spinner programmed as shown
index card labeled with whole numbers and/or decimals
paper

A student writes a number from the card on her paper as shown. She spins the spinner, multiplies the chosen number by the number spun, and records the product. She repeats the steps, using a different number from the card and adding each new product to the existing sum until the total exceeds 100,000. If she uses all the numbers on the card before she reaches the target, she repeats them in any order as many times as needed.

Ava

3.51 x 10 = 35.1	35.1 +40
4 x 10 = 40	75.1 +60,000
60 x 1,000 = 60,000	60,075.1 +700
0.7 x 1,000 = 700	60,775.1 +1,000
10 x 100 = 1,000	61,775.1 +1,200
12 x 100 = 1,200	62,975.1 +914
0.914 x 1,000 = 914	63,889.1 +3,510
3.51 x 1,000 = 3,510	67,399.1 +6,000
60 x 100 = 6,000	73,399.1 +12,000
12 x 1,000 = 12,000	85,399.1 +10,000
10 x 1,000 = 10,000	95,399.1 +400
4 x 100 = 400	95,469.1 + 70
0.7 x 100 = 70	95,560.5 +91.4
0.914 x 100 = 91.4	95,560.5 +6,000
60 x 100 = 6,000	101,560.5

4	3.51
	0.7
60	12
10	0.914

×10
×100
×1,000

Feed the Pooches

Weight

Materials:
5 paper lunch bags labeled as shown
disposable cup
1-lb. bag of dried beans
balance scale
gram weights

A student selects a bag and places it in a pan on one side of the scale. In the other pan, he places weights equal to the weight written on the bag. Using the cup as a scoop, he adds or removes beans until the bag's contents equal the labeled weight. He repeats the steps with each remaining bag.

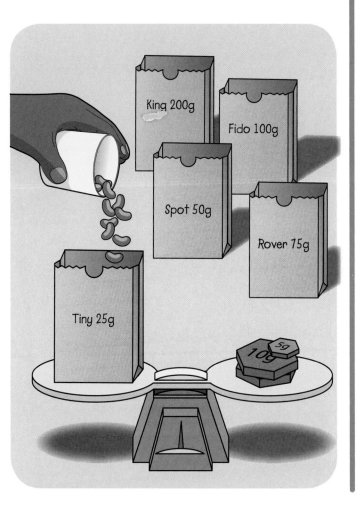

Junior Analysts

Line graphs

Materials:
tables of data that show change over time
paper
red and green colored pencils

Tables can be cut from magazines or photocopied from students' math textbooks.

A student selects a table and uses its data to make a line graph on her paper. She uses the red pencil to circle the point representing the graph's greatest value and the green pencil to circle the point representing the least value. Then she writes a title that summarizes the data.

Month	Games Sold (in Thousands)
January	50
February	100
March	75
April	100
May	125
June	150
July	225
August	100
September	25
October	75
November	125
December	175

Sales Sizzle in July — Emma
Number of Video Games Sold
(in Thousands)

Zigzag Math

Decimals

Materials:
student copies of page 87
10 index cards labeled with different decimals as shown

A student chooses a card. He uses the number on the card as the starting number on his paper. Then he performs the indicated operation and writes the sum or difference in the next circle until he arrives at Finish. To check his work, he verifies that the numbers in the circles at his paper's left and right edges match his starting number.

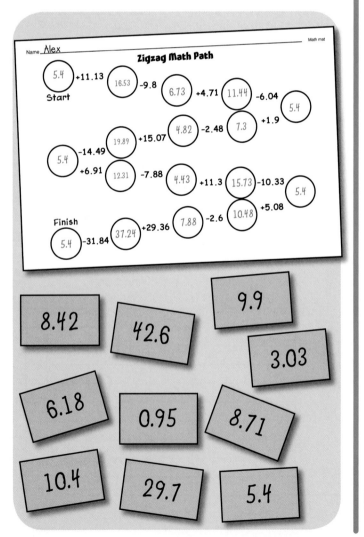

Break It Down!

Multiplication

Materials:
index cards labeled with multiplication problems
paper

A student chooses a multiplication problem and copies it on her paper. She uses expanded form to rewrite the problem as an addition problem. She then multiplies the simpler problems and adds the products together to get a final answer. She repeats the steps until she solves all the problems.

$$398 \times 9 =$$

$$38 \times 42 =$$

Crystal

$398 \times 9 =$

$(300 \times 9) + (90 \times 9) + (8 \times 9) =$

$2,700 + 810 + 72 = 3,582$

2,700
810
+ 72
3,582

$38 \times 42 =$

$(30 + 8) \times (40 + 2) =$

$(30 \times 40) + (30 \times 2) + (8 \times 40) + (8 \times 2) =$

$1,200 + 60 + 320 + 16 = 1,596$

1,200
60
320
+ 16
1,596

Measure and Match

Length

Materials:
copy of the cards on page 88, cut apart
ruler

A student selects a line segment card and measures the segment's length from dot to dot. Then he finds the corresponding clue card and sets the matching cards aside. He continues to measure and match until all the cards are paired correctly.

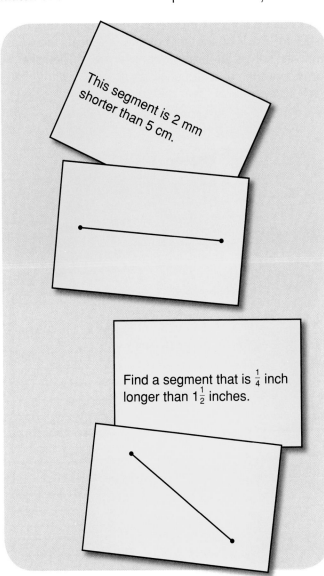

This segment is 2 mm shorter than 5 cm.

Find a segment that is $\frac{1}{4}$ inch longer than $1\frac{1}{2}$ inches.

Which Birthday?

Algebraic expressions

Materials:
construction paper (one sheet per student)
markers

A student folds her paper to make a birthday card for a friend or family member. On the front, she writes a greeting that includes an exponent or a variable. On the inside, she writes a message that includes the expression's solution. Then she decorates the card.

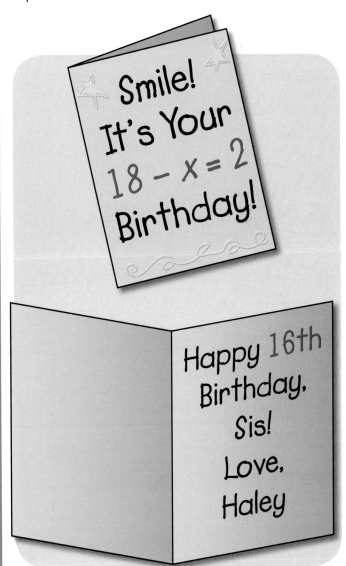

Smile! It's Your $18 - x = 2$ Birthday!

Happy 16th Birthday, Sis! Love, Haley

Snaking Along

Multiplication

Materials:
student copies of the hundred chart on page 89
colored pencil
paper
calculator

A student circles two adjacent numbers at the top of his chart with a colored pencil. He writes the numbers on his paper as a multiplication problem and finds the product. Then he circles two different numbers, making sure one number in the pair is vertically, horizontally, or diagonally adjacent to one of the last numbers circled. He continues to circle number pairs and find their product until he works his way to the chart's bottom row. Then he checks his work with the calculator.

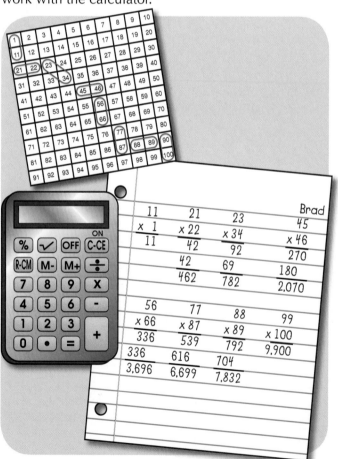

Fishy Products

Multiplying decimals

Materials:
plastic cup
copy of the color problems chart on page 89
3 different-colored index cards, cut into sixths and labeled with problems (without answers) from the chart
paper

A student turns the problem chart facedown and chooses a color of cards to fish from the cup. She works that color's six problems on her paper and then fishes for cards of another color. She repeats the steps until she solves all three sets of problems. Then she turns over the chart and checks her work, noting that each set's products are the same.

Up and Down the Scale

Temperature

Materials:
student copies of the thermometers on page 89
2 dice of different colors in a paper bag
colored pencil
paper
scissors
glue

A student cuts out, folds, and glues his thermometers back-to-back. He also decides which die will increase and which will decrease the temperature when rolled. Without looking, he draws a die from the bag; then he rolls the die and colorfully marks a new Fahrenheit temperature above or below Start as shown. He also records the temperature on his paper. He repeats the steps until he marks and records a total of ten temperature changes for each thermometer.

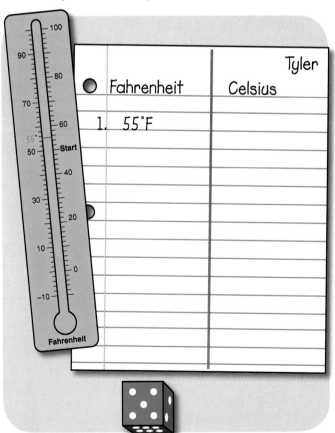

Category Detective

Angles

Materials:
pattern blocks
paper
crayons

A student divides her paper into columns and labels them as shown. She classifies the pattern blocks according to the type(s) of angles they contain. Then she traces and labels each pattern block in the appropriate column(s) and outlines the corresponding angle.

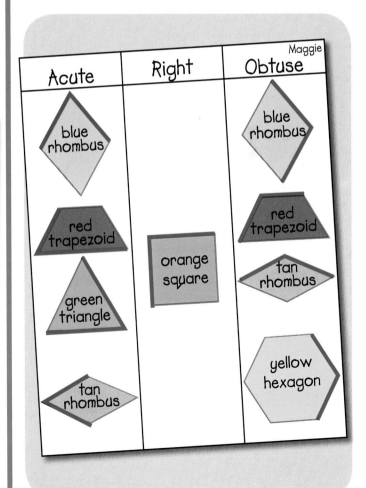

Simply "Mathical"

Two-step problems

Materials:
list shown
paper

A student selects three different facts from the list. He uses the facts to write and solve ten math problems like the one shown.

Year Columbus first sailed to America: 1492
Number of ships Columbus had when he set sail: 3
Year Neil Armstrong set foot on the moon: 1969
Boiling point of water on Fahrenheit scale: 212
Freezing point of water on Fahrenheit scale: 32
Year American colonies won independence from England: 1776
Number of original American colonies: 13
Number of letters in the alphabet: 26
Number of feet in a mile: 5,280
Number of inches in a foot: 12
Number of inches in a yard: 36
Normal body temperature in degrees Fahrenheit: 98.6
Number of days in January: 31

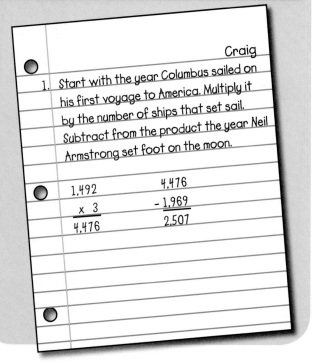

Craig

1. Start with the year Columbus sailed on his first voyage to America. Multiply it by the number of ships that set sail. Subtract from the product the year Neil Armstrong set foot on the moon.

$$\begin{array}{r} 1{,}492 \\ \times\ 3 \\ \hline 4{,}476 \end{array} \qquad \begin{array}{r} 4{,}476 \\ -\ 1{,}969 \\ \hline 2{,}507 \end{array}$$

Bottle Cap Dilemma

Decimals

Materials:
student copies of the recording sheet on page 90
4 plastic bottle caps labeled as shown
index card labeled as shown

A student arranges the bottle caps on the recording sheet's circles to discover which letter represents each decimal. He records the decimals at the bottom of the recording sheet and checks his work with the index card.

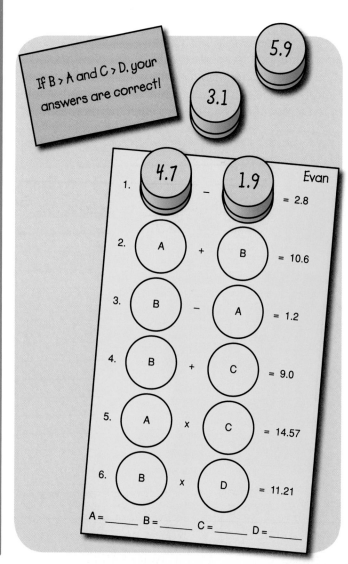

If B > A and C > D, your answers are correct!

5.9

3.1

Evan

1. 4.7 − 1.9 = 2.8
2. A + B = 10.6
3. B − A = 1.2
4. B + C = 9.0
5. A × C = 14.57
6. B × D = 11.21

A = _____ B = _____ C = _____ D = _____

Roll and Race

Perimeter

For partners

Materials:
2 dice
graph paper

A student rolls the dice and announces a two-digit number with the numbers rolled. Each partner then races to draw on his graph paper a shape whose perimeter is that number. The first student to finish says, "Done!" His partner checks his work. If it is correct, the drawer earns a point. If not, the round continues until there is a winner. Play continues, with partners taking turns to form the numbers, until time is up or ten figures have been drawn.

Your Average Pizza

Mean, median, mode, range

Materials:
student copies of page 91
crayons

On each pizza circle, a student draws several toppings of each kind shown on the key. Based on her drawings, she completes the table and the chart. Then she refers to her data to answer the questions.

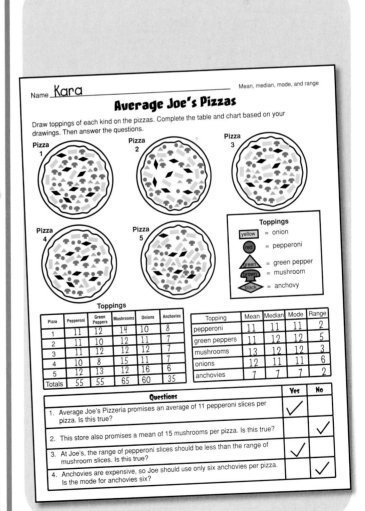

Name Kara   Mean, median, mode, and range

Average Joe's Pizzas

Draw toppings of each kind on the pizzas. Complete the table and chart based on your drawings. Then answer the questions.

Toppings key:
yellow = onion
red = pepperoni
green = green pepper
brown = mushroom
black = anchovy

Toppings

Pizza	Pepperoni	Green Peppers	Mushrooms	Onions	Anchovies
1	11	12	14	10	8
2	11	10	12	11	7
3	11	12	12	12	7
4	10	8	15	11	7
5	12	13	12	16	6
Totals	55	55	65	60	35

Topping	Mean	Median	Mode	Range
pepperoni	11	11	11	2
green peppers	11	12	12	5
mushrooms	13	12	12	3
onions	12	11	11	6
anchovies	7	7	7	2

Questions	Yes	No
1. Average Joe's Pizzeria promises an average of 11 pepperoni slices per pizza. Is this true?	✓	
2. This store also promises a mean of 15 mushrooms per pizza. Is this true?		✓
3. At Joe's, the range of pepperoni slices should be less than the range of mushroom slices. Is this true?	✓	
4. Anchovies are expensive, so Joe should use only six anchovies per pizza. Is the mode for anchovies six?		✓

Number Trios

Relating multiplication and division

Materials:
copy of the number cards on page 90, cut apart
paper

A student selects one card at a time and uses its numbers to write a multiplication riddle and a division riddle as shown. He continues in this manner until he has written 12 math riddles. Then he solves the riddles, showing his work on his paper.

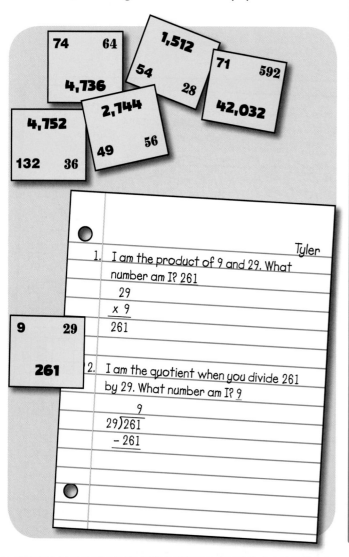

Daffy Division

1-digit and 2-digit divisors

Materials:
copy of the division problems on page 92,
  mounted on construction paper (if desired)
paper
calculator

A student solves each division problem on her paper, rounding the quotient to the nearest whole number if necessary. Then she uses the calculator to check her work.

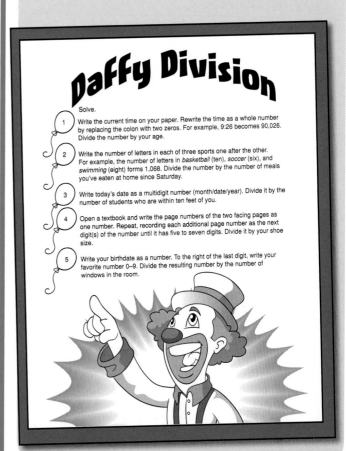

Go, Team!

Area

Materials:
poster labeled as shown
8 sticky notes placed as shown
paper

A student uses the formula *area = length* x *width* to find the area of each playing site listed on the poster. After he solves a problem on his paper, he lifts the corresponding sticky note to check his answer.

Playing Site	Length	Width	Area
football field	100 yd.	53.5 yd.	5,350 sq. yd.
basketball court (largest)	94 ft.	50 ft.	
basketball court (smallest)	74 ft.	42 ft.	
soccer field (largest)	130 yd.	100 yd.	
soccer field (smallest)	100 yd.	50 yd.	
tennis court (singles)	78 ft.	27 ft.	
tennis court (doubles)	78 ft.	36 ft.	
table tennis table	108 in.	60 in.	6,480 sq. in.

Domino Dots

Patterning

Materials:
dominoes
paper

A student turns the dominoes facedown and shuffles them. Next, she draws two dominoes and turns them faceup. She writes on her paper in any order the four numbers represented on the dominoes. She determines the numbers' pattern and then writes its next three numbers to extend it. She repeats the steps with different dominoes until she has written five number patterns.

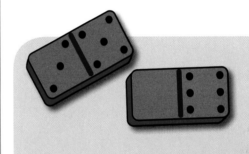

Numbers	Pattern	Next Three Numbers
3, 0, 6, 5	subtract 3, add 6, subtract 1	2, 8, 7
		Patti

Set 13

Hit the Target

Estimation

For partners

Materials:
poster, labeled as shown
calculator
paper

Each player selects from the poster a product as his target and one factor and then records the numbers on his paper. He enters the factor on the calculator, multiplies it by any number he wishes, and records the product on his paper. He repeats the steps two more times, trying to get closer to his target each time. Then he circles on his paper the product closest to his target. The player whose circled product is closer to his target earns five points. The first student to earn 50 points wins.

Target Products

573	764
3,640	10,975
21,345	3,250
2,359	1,039
619	384
812	5,492

Factors

526	22
46	51
16	6
218	37
249	102
54	9

Alan

Target product: 10,975
Factor: 249

249 X 12 = 2,988
249 X 60 = 14,940
249 X 40 = (9,960)

Make a Match

Decimals

Materials:
10 sentence strips labeled as shown
5 index cards labeled with equal signs
paper

A student solves on her paper each problem from the sentence strips. Then, using the products as a guide, she arranges the sentence strips and index cards to form five true equations.

1.3 x 0.4	=	26 x 0.02
0.002 x 12	=	0.08 x 0.3
10 x 0.02	=	0.4 x 0.5
24.8 x 0.03	=	2.4 x 0.31
2.4 x 0.39	=	0.18 x 5.2

Thirsty No More

Capacity

Materials:
paper slips labeled with the units shown
disposable cup to hold the slips
die
paper

A student labels three columns on his paper as shown. He rolls the die and draws a slip to determine an amount of liquid. He decides whether that amount would satisfy the thirst of a giant, a human, or a pixie and records the amount under the appropriate column. He returns the slip to the cup and repeats the steps until he has recorded five amounts.

Customary	Metric
gallon	liter
quart	milliliter
pint	
cup	
tablespoon	
teaspoon	

milliliter

Colin

Giant	Human	Pixie
6 gallons	2 pints	1 milliliter

Twenty Draws

Probability

Materials:
20 color tiles or cubes in several colors
small paper bag
paper

Without looking, a student draws a tile or cube from the bag. She records the item's color on her paper and makes a tally mark. She returns the item to the bag, shakes it, and draws another item. After 20 such draws, she uses her data to guess the most common color in the bag. Then she empties the bag, sorts the items by color, and counts the number in each pile to check her answer.

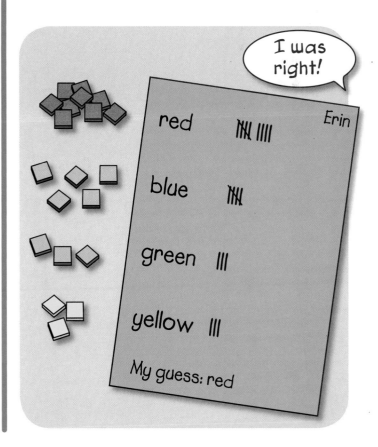

I was right!

Erin

red	⦀⦀ ||||
blue	⦀⦀
green	|||
yellow	|||

My guess: red

Finding Lost Digits

Multiplication

Materials:
problem cards with blank boxes
paper

A student selects a card. She copies the problem on her paper. Then she solves the problem by writing numbers in the boxes to make the problem true. She continues solving problems in this manner as time allows.

How Close Can You Get?

Estimation

For partners

Materials:
labeled sticky notes affixed to a poster as shown
calculator
paper

Each student selects a sticky note from each section and affixes the notes to his paper. He enters the dividend on the calculator, divides it by a compatible number or a multiple of ten, and records the quotient on his paper. He repeats the steps twice more, trying to get closer to his target each time. Then he circles the quotient on his paper that is closest to his target. The partner whose circled quotient is closer to his target earns three points. The first student to earn 21 points wins.

Target Quotients		Dividends	
18	11	273	487
15	83	613	303
5	44	278	2,487
80	55	159	148
20	10	429	538
25	9	4,646	941

Feeding the Animals

Elapsed time

Materials:
4 paper strips labeled as shown
envelope labeled as shown
paper

A student copies the starting time on his paper. He draws a paper strip from the bag and adds to the starting time the time it takes to feed the animals named on the strip. He continues pulling strips and adding each indicated time to the previous answer until all strips have been drawn. Then he labels his final answer "Finish."

Otters
15 minutes

Penguins
22 minutes

Elephants
34 minutes

Lions
26 minutes

Feeding Time at the Zoo

Start: 8:00 AM

Jeff

```
              8:00
Start        +:15
Otters        8:15
             +:22
Penguins      8:37
             +:34
Elephants     9:11
             +:26
Lions         9:37
Finish
```

Fold It!

Lines of symmetry

Materials:
cutouts of shapes and letters

A student selects several cutouts. She labels each one with her name and a guess about the number of lines of symmetry it has. Next, she folds each cutout to determine its lines of symmetry. She traces each line of symmetry she finds and then records the total number found.

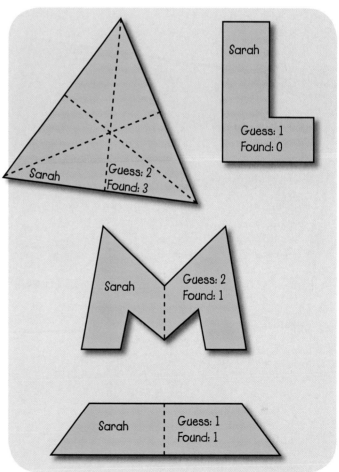

Sarah

Guess: 1
Found: 0

Sarah

Guess: 2
Found: 3

Sarah

Guess: 2
Found: 1

Sarah

Guess: 1
Found: 1

Heading Home

Multiplication

Materials:
copy of the gameboard on page 93
index cards, each labeled with a
    different problem
2 game markers
penny
calculator
paper

For
partners

Each student chooses a game trail and takes a turn drawing a card, solving the problem on his paper, and using the calculator to check his answer. If his answer is correct, he flips the coin and moves his game marker accordingly (heads = one space, tails = two spaces). The first player to reach Home wins.

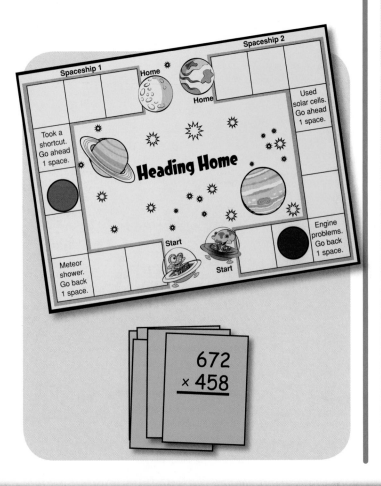

Weather Trends

Averages

Materials:
paper strips labeled with 5 temperatures as shown
paper

A student chooses a card. She adds the temperatures together and divides their sum by five. She rounds the quotient to the nearest whole number if necessary.

Day	1	2	3	4	5
Temperature °F	70°	65°	74°	79°	73°

Day	1	2	3	4	5
Temperature °F	46°	51°	39°	37°	40°

Ellen

```
  70              72 R1 = 72°
  65           5)361
  74            - 35
  79             11
+ 73            - 10
 361              1
```

```
  46              42 R3 = 43°
  51           5)213
  39            - 20
  37             13
+ 40            - 10
 213              3
```

Weighing In

Weight

Materials:
objects to weigh
balance and weights
chart labeled as shown
paper

Possible objects include a seashell, 6 Unifix cubes, 10 crayons, 5 craft sticks, and a plastic ruler.

A student selects an object or a set of objects and uses the balance and weights to find the weight. He copies the chart on his paper and writes the object's name by the matching weight. He repeats the steps with each object or set of objects.

Object	Weight
?	30 g
?	25 g
?	50 g
?	10 g
?	20 g

Randy

Object	Weight
seashell	30 g
Unifix cubes	25 g
crayons	50 g
craft sticks	10 g
ruler	20 g

Find Four

Algebraic expressions

Materials:
copy of the instructions on page 93
2 library pocket cards labeled as shown and mounted on poster board with the instructions
index cards (two per student)

A student studies the examples on the instructions. She follows the steps to label her cards and then places the cards in the appropriate pockets on the poster board. At a later time, the student matches the expressions to their solutions.

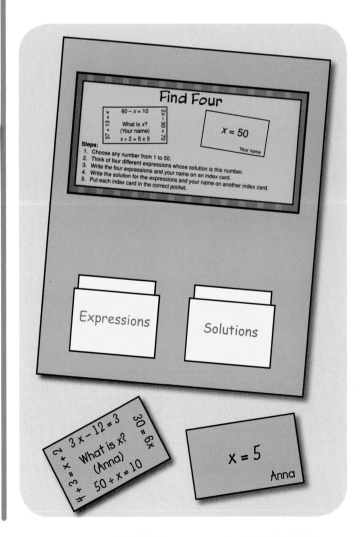

Find Four

$60 - x = 10$
$37 + 13 = x$
What is x? (Your name)
$x \div 2 = 5 \times 5$
$2 \times 90 = 70$

$x = 50$
Your name

Steps:
1. Choose any number from 1 to 50.
2. Think of four different expressions whose solution is this number.
3. Write the four expressions and your name on an index card.
4. Write the solution for the expressions and your name on another index card.
5. Put each index card in the correct pocket.

Expressions

Solutions

$3x - 12 = 3$
$4 + x = 2$
What is x? (Anna)
$30 = 6x$
$50 \div x = 10$

$x = 5$
Anna

Grocery Shopping

Problem solving

Materials:
grocery store receipt glued to paper
list of questions, like the one shown
paper

A student selects five questions from the list. He uses the store receipt to answer the questions and then writes his answers on his paper.

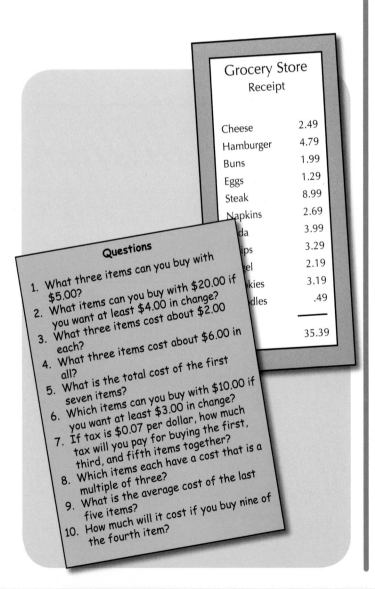

Grocery Store
Receipt

Cheese	2.49
Hamburger	4.79
Buns	1.99
Eggs	1.29
Steak	8.99
Napkins	2.69
da	3.99
ips	3.29
el	2.19
kies	3.19
dles	.49
	35.39

Questions

1. What three items can you buy with $5.00?
2. What items can you buy with $20.00 if you want at least $4.00 in change?
3. What three items cost about $2.00 each?
4. What three items cost about $6.00 in all?
5. What is the total cost of the first seven items?
6. Which items can you buy with $10.00 if you want at least $3.00 in change?
7. If tax is $0.07 per dollar, how much tax will you pay for buying the first, third, and fifth items together?
8. Which items each have a cost that is a multiple of three?
9. What is the average cost of the last five items?
10. How much will it cost if you buy nine of the fourth item?

Look at the Question

Remainders

Materials:
index cards numbered and labeled with word problems
paper

A student reads the problem on each card, paying particular attention to the question. As she solves each problem on her paper, she decides whether to drop the remainder, round the quotient to the next greater number, or use the remainder as part of her answer.

1. Seven of the 230 new library books will be displayed each week. For how many weeks will new books be displayed?

Amber

1.
$$7\overline{)230} \quad 32\text{ R}6$$
$$-21$$
$$20$$
$$-14$$
$$6$$

33 weeks
Round to the next greater whole number.

Bingo Solitaire

Temperature

Materials:
copy of "Find the Match" on page 94 with a paper circle
    taped over the key as shown
game markers
paper

A student draws a bingo board on his paper. In each square, he writes a different letter of the alphabet, using all but one letter. Next, he follows the directions on the clue sheet until he covers five letters in a row on his bingo board. Then he lifts the circle covering the answer key to check his answers.

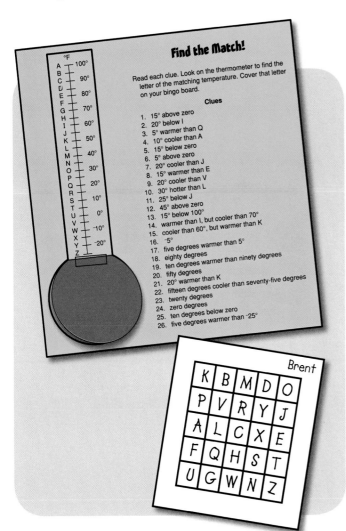

Find the Match!

Read each clue. Look on the thermometer to find the letter of the matching temperature. Cover that letter on your bingo board.

Clues

1. 15° above zero
2. 20° below I
3. 5° warmer than Q
4. 10° cooler than A
5. 15° below zero
6. 5° above zero
7. 20° cooler than J
8. 15° warmer than E
9. 20° cooler than V
10. 30° hotter than L
11. 25° below J
12. 45° above zero
13. 15° below 100°
14. warmer than I, but cooler than 70°
15. cooler than 60°, but warmer than K
16. -5°
17. five degrees warmer than 5°
18. eighty degrees
19. ten degrees warmer than ninety degrees
20. fifty degrees
21. 20° warmer than K
22. fifteen degrees cooler than seventy-five degrees
23. twenty degrees
24. zero degrees
25. ten degrees below zero
26. five degrees warmer than -25°

Brent bingo board:
K	B	M	D	O
P	V	R	Y	J
A	L	C	X	E
F	Q	H	S	T
U	G	W	N	Z

Track the Scores!

Stem-and-leaf plot

Materials:
lists of two-digit numbers, like the ones shown
paper

A student selects a list and orders its numbers on her paper from least to greatest. She draws a T chart on her paper and labels the columns as shown. Under the stem column, she writes the numbers' tens digits. Under the leaf column, she writes the numbers' ones digits in rows, ordering the digits from least to greatest. Then she chooses a different list and makes a stem-and-leaf plot to represent its data.

Reggie's Test Scores

76
85
91
77
86
92
77
88
93

Cougars' Basketball Scores

76
80
90
77
82
90
78
83
91
79
85
92
79

Cougars' Basketball Scores
76, 77, 78, 79, 79, 79
80, 82, 83, 85, 85, 86, 88, 89
90, 90, 91, 92, 93, 98

Megan

Stem	Leaf
7	6 7 8 9 9 9
8	0 2 3 5 5 6 8 9
9	0 0 1 2 3 8

Reggie's Test Scores
76, 77, 77
85, 86, 88
91, 92, 93

Stem	Leaf
7	6 7 7
8	5 6 8
9	1 2 3

Storybook Fractions

Parts of a whole or set

Materials:
picture book with a sticky note flagging one page
list of fraction questions, like the one shown, about the
    flagged page

A student opens the book to the flagged page. He
answers the list of questions, writing each answer on
his paper in its simplest form.

1. What fraction of the words on the flagged page are nouns?
2. What fraction of the words on the flagged page have two syllables?
3. What fraction of the words on the flagged page begin with the letter a?
4. What fraction of the sentences on the flagged page are exclamations?
5. What fraction of the words on the flagged page begin with capital letters?
6. What fraction of the words on the flagged page are verbs?
7. What fraction of the sentences on the flagged page are statements?
8. What fraction of the words on the flagged page are adjectives?
9. What fraction of the sentences on the flagged page ask questions?
10. What fraction of the sentences on the flagged page contain quotation marks?

Out
and
About

Quotient Patterns

Decimals

Materials:
sentence strip labeled front and back as shown and
    laminated
wipe-off marker
paper

A student solves on her paper each of the division problems. If her quotient matches the one on
the strip, she draws a circle around the problem with
the marker. If not, she draws a box. After solving all
the problems, she checks her work by comparing her
shape pattern with the one on the back of the strip.

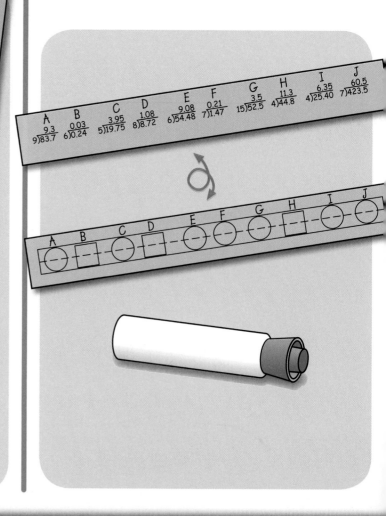

Obstacle Course

Measuring length

For partners

Materials:
die
ruler
blank paper

Each student draws a start box at the top of his paper and a finish box at the bottom. Next, he draws three to five objects on his paper in various locations. Each child then takes a turn rolling the die and drawing a line segment (horizontal or vertical) from his start box equal in length (inches or centimeters) to the number rolled. Students continue in this manner, each trying to reach his finish box first without hitting an obstacle or running out of room to draw.

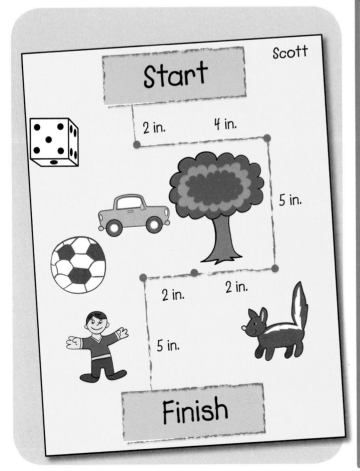

Give Me Five!

Variables

Materials:
tagboard hand cutout(s), labeled front and back as shown
paper

A student selects a hand cutout. She solves each equation, locates the matching answer on a finger of the cutout, and writes her answer on her paper. She repeats the steps with each hand.

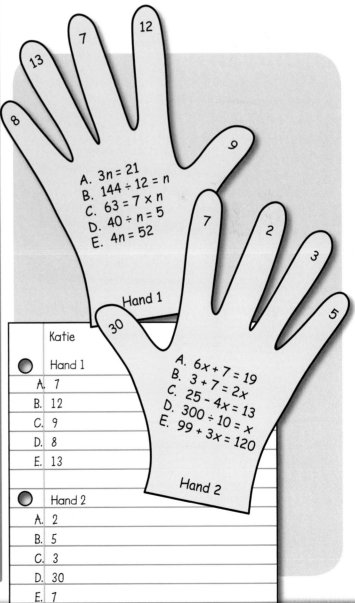

Hand 1
A. 3n = 21
B. 144 ÷ 12 = n
C. 63 = 7 × n
D. 40 ÷ n = 5
E. 4n = 52

Hand 2
A. 6x + 7 = 19
B. 3 + 7 = 2x
C. 25 − 4x = 13
D. 300 ÷ 10 = x
E. 99 + 3x = 120

	Katie
○	Hand 1
A.	7
B.	12
C.	9
D.	8
E.	13
○	Hand 2
A.	2
B.	5
C.	3
D.	30
E.	7

It's in the Bag!

Fractions

Materials:
small paper bag filled with assorted attribute blocks
  or die-cut shapes
list of questions, like the one shown, related to
  the bag's contents
paper

A student empties the bag and uses its contents to help him answer the questions. He records his answers on his paper, writing each fraction in its simplest form. Then he puts the items back in the bag.

Questions

1. What fraction of the items are red?
2. What fraction of the items are blue?
3. What fraction of the items are yellow?
4. What fraction of the items have a circular shape?
5. What fraction of the items have a square or rectangular shape?
6. What fraction of the items have a triangular shape?
7. What fraction of the items have a hexagonal shape?
8. What fraction of the squares and rectangles are blue?
9. What fraction of the triangles are yellow?
10. What fraction of the hexagonal items are red?

Matt

1. $^9/_{20}$
2. $^6/_{20}$, or $^3/_{10}$
3. $^5/_{20}$, or $^1/_4$
4. $^1/_{20}$
5. $^{10}/_{20}$, or $^1/_2$
6. $^7/_{20}$
7. $^2/_{20}$, or $^1/_{10}$
8. $^3/_{10}$
9. $^2/_7$
10. $^0/_2$

Places, Please!

Fractions

Materials:
file folder with library pocket glued inside, as shown
index card cut into seven strips, labeled as shown
2 copies of the fraction number line from page 94,
  cut out, one labeled as shown and both glued
  inside the folder as shown
strip of construction paper, taped over one number
  line as shown

A student removes a fraction strip from the library pocket. She places the strip above its matching equivalent fraction on the uncovered number line. She continues until she has placed all the strips. Then she lifts the paper flap to check her work.

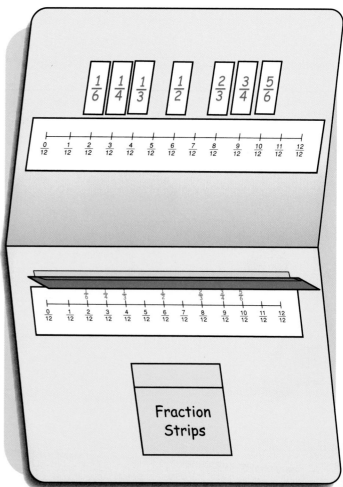

Construction Site

Area and perimeter

Materials:
tagboard copy of the cards on page 95, cut apart, folded, and taped as shown
5 x 5 Geoboard
rubber bands
dot paper

A student selects a task card. He constructs on the Geoboard a figure that matches the instructions on the card. He records his design on the dot paper. Then he turns the card over to check his work. He repeats the steps until he has completed all the tasks.

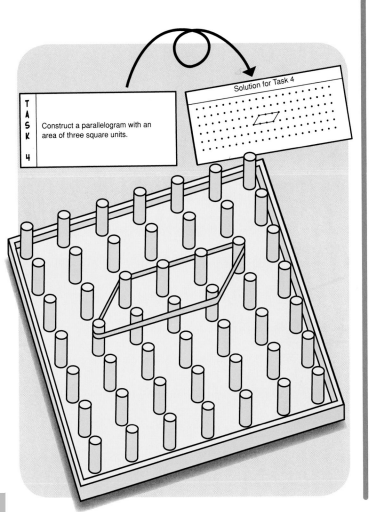

TASK 4: Construct a parallelogram with an area of three square units.

Solution for Task 4

Geometry Reinforcer

Polygons and angles

Materials:
construction paper with hole reinforcers randomly placed on it, laminated
wipe-off marker
paper

A student uses the marker to draw lines on the construction paper to connect the hole reinforcers. She connects as many reinforcers as she wishes to create a design that includes both angles and polygons. After she writes a paragraph about the figures she created, she wipes the lines off the paper.

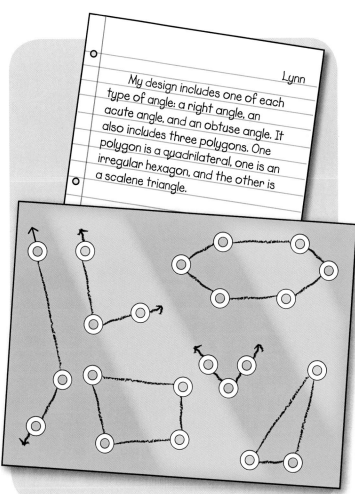

Lynn

My design includes one of each type of angle: a right angle, an acute angle, and an obtuse angle. It also includes three polygons. One polygon is a quadrilateral, one is an irregular hexagon, and the other is a scalene triangle.

Any Way You Slice It!

Fractions

Materials:
7 index cards labeled with the fractions shown
paper circle divided into 12 equal parts
crayons
paper

A student selects a fraction card and draws a circle on his paper. He divides the circle into the same number of parts as the fraction's denominator and colors the same number of parts as the numerator. Next, he draws a second circle. He divides it into 12 parts, like the sample, and colors it to match the colored area of his first circle. Then he writes an equation that represents his drawings. He repeats the steps with each card.

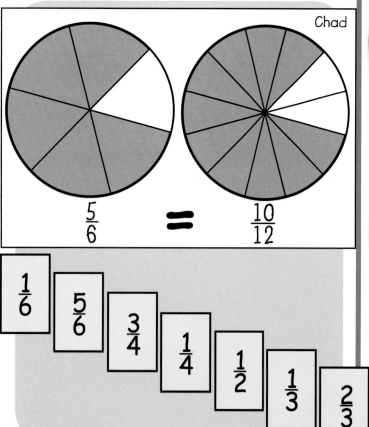

Chad

$$\frac{5}{6} = \frac{10}{12}$$

$\frac{1}{6}$ $\frac{5}{6}$ $\frac{3}{4}$ $\frac{1}{4}$ $\frac{1}{2}$ $\frac{1}{3}$ $\frac{2}{3}$

Sort the Apples

Rounding fractions

Materials:
12 apple cutouts, each labeled with a different fraction
3 paper plates labeled as shown
paper

A student selects an apple cutout and decides whether its fraction is closest to zero, one-half, or one. She places the apple on the matching plate. When all the apples are sorted, she records her work on her paper.

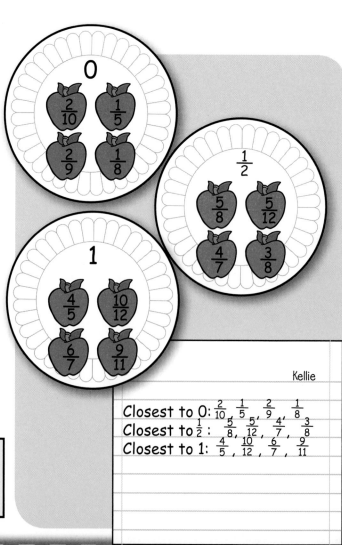

Kellie

Closest to 0: $\frac{2}{10}$ $\frac{1}{5}$ $\frac{2}{9}$ $\frac{1}{8}$
Closest to $\frac{1}{2}$: $\frac{5}{8}$, $\frac{5}{12}$, $\frac{4}{7}$, $\frac{3}{8}$
Closest to 1: $\frac{4}{5}$, $\frac{10}{12}$, $\frac{6}{7}$, $\frac{9}{11}$

Multiply or Divide?

Capacity

Materials:
index cards labeled with problems like the ones shown
2 paper plates labeled as shown
paper

A student selects a card and decides whether to multiply or divide to change its units of capacity. He places the card on the corresponding plate. When all the cards are on the plates, he solves each problem on his paper.

X

5 c. = _____ fl. oz.

÷

4 c. = _____ pt.

			Colin
	Multiply	Divide	
	5 c. = 40 fl. oz.	4 c. = 2 pt.	
	1 qt. = 4 c.	20 qt. = 5 gal.	

X Colors the Spot!

Line plot

Materials:
small bag of colorful paper squares
colored pencils or crayons
paper

A student takes a handful of paper squares from the bag. She sorts the pieces by color and constructs a line plot on her paper to represent her findings. Then she calculates the data's mean, median, mode, and range.

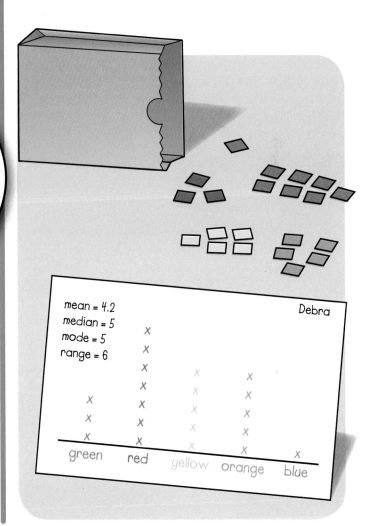

mean = 4.2
median = 5
mode = 5
range = 6

Debra

green   red   yellow   orange   blue

Venn Mats

Factors and multiples

Materials:
large sheet of construction paper (mat)
    labeled front and back as shown
2 small resealable bags, labeled as shown,
    filled with 1" paper squares labeled
    with the numbers shown
paper

Venn diagram 1: 1, 2, 3, 4, 5, 6, 7, 8, 9, 11, 12, 15, 18,
    21, 23, 24
Venn diagram 2: 1, 3, 5, 6, 7, 8, 9, 10, 12, 14, 15, 16,
    17, 18, 20, 21, 22, 24, 30, 36

A student removes the cards from the Venn diagram 1 bag and places them in the correct location on the Venn diagram 1 side of the mat, setting aside any cards that don't apply. He records his work on his paper and returns the cards to the bag. Then he flips the mat and repeats the steps using the numbers in the Venn diagram 2 bag.

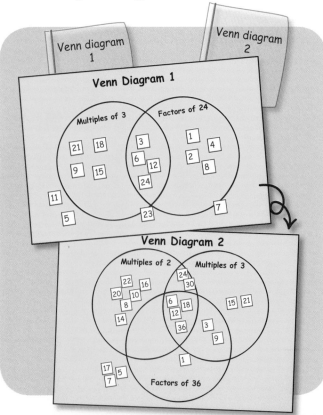

Puzzle Solver

Fractions

Materials:
copy of page 96, cut apart and placed in
    a small resealable bag
file folder labeled "Answer Key," with a
    copy of page 96 glued inside as shown

A student removes the puzzle pieces from the bag, shuffles the pieces, and arranges them to form a 4 x 4 square. She makes sure that the fractions on all sides of adjoining pieces are equivalent. She then checks her work against the key before returning the pieces to the bag.

Check the Schedule

Problem solving

Materials:
copy of the activity chart from page 97
index cards, each labeled with a number of minutes:
    500, 600, 700, 800
paper

A student divides a sheet of paper into seven sections and labels each one with a day of the week. Next, he selects a card and looks at the chart. Then he lists on his paper activities he could do during the week while trying to achieve a total activity time as close to the time on his card as possible.

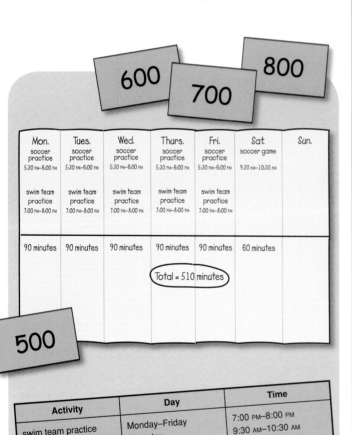

Activity	Day	Time
swim team practice	Monday–Friday	7:00 PM–8:00 PM
soccer game	Saturday	9:30 AM–10:30 AM
soccer practice	Monday–Friday	5:30 PM–6:00 PM
tennis lesson	Saturday and Sunday	6:00 PM–6:30 PM
hiking club	Saturday	1:00 PM–6:00 PM
bowling team	Tuesday and Thursday	8:00 PM–9:00 PM

Code Breakers

Number patterns

Materials:
copies of the treasure chest and key patterns
    on page 97, labeled with patterns and
    codes like the ones shown
paper

A student selects a treasure chest, identifies its number pattern, and places it next to the key with the matching code. She copies the code and series of numbers onto her paper. Then she writes the pattern's next three numbers to extend it. She repeats the steps with each treasure chest.

Pattern	Code
10, 17, 16, 23, 22, 29, 28, 35	+7, −1
3, 9.5, 9, 15.5, 15, 21.5, 21, 27.5	+6.5, −0.5
12, 20, 19.75, 27.75, 27.5, 35.5, 35.25, 43.25	+8, −0.25
70, 75, 62, 67, 54, 59, 46, 51	+5, −13
83, 67, 69.5, 53.5, 56, 40, 42.5, 26.5	−16, +2.5
12, $12\frac{1}{2}$, $12\frac{1}{4}$, $12\frac{3}{4}$, $12\frac{1}{2}$, 13, $12\frac{3}{4}$, $13\frac{1}{4}$	$+\frac{1}{2}$, $-\frac{1}{4}$

Simplify It!

Fractions

For partners

Materials:
list of denominators, like the one shown
2 dice
paper

Each student draws three columns on his paper and labels them as shown. Then the partners select a denominator for the round. One player rolls the dice, uses the sum of the numbers rolled as the numerator, and then writes on his paper the resulting fraction in its simplest form. If he is correct, he earns a point and his partner takes a turn. If not, his partner gets a chance to earn the point. The first player to earn ten points wins. Then the pair chooses a different denominator for the next round.

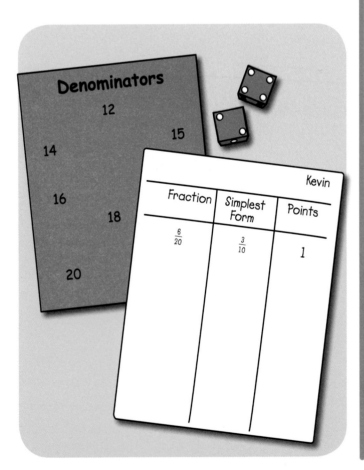

Denominators

12

15

14

16

18

20

Kevin

Fraction	Simplest Form	Points
$\frac{6}{20}$	$\frac{3}{10}$	1

"Tree-mendous"

Prime factorization

Materials:
student copies of the tree patterns on page 97 (three per student)
list of the ten numbers shown
black, green, and brown crayons

A student labels a tree top with any number from 50 to 100 that is not on the list. Beginning with 2 (if her number is even) or 3 (if it is odd), she factors her number, drawing lines between rows as shown, until all the factors are prime numbers. Then she colors her tree. She repeats the steps with two more trees.

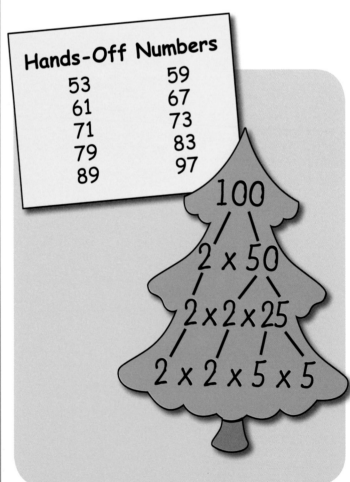

Hands-Off Numbers

53	59
61	67
71	73
79	83
89	97

100
2 x 50
2 x 2 x 25
2 x 2 x 5 x 5

Picture-Perfect

Geometry

Materials:
copies of the cube pattern on page 98,
    labeled with geometric drawings
paper

A student selects a cube and writes on his paper the name of the drawing on each of the cube's six faces. Then he selects a second cube and repeats the process.

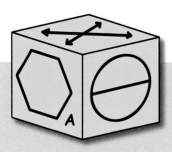

Jared

Cube A: intersecting lines, hexagon, diameter of a circle, trapezoid, acute angle, cube

Scenic Degrees

Angles

Materials:
color-coded list of angle measurements,
    like the one shown
protractor
crayons or colored pencils
paper

A student draws on her paper an illustration that includes angles of the sizes listed, using the protractor to size the angles. Then she colors the angles by the code.

Angle Measurement	Color
20°	yellow
30°	green
40°	blue
50°	purple
65°	orange
75°	brown
90°	pink
100°	red
130°	gray
145°	black

Ashley

Sports-Score Fractions

Simplest form

Materials:
team scores cut from a newspaper, mounted
    on construction paper
paper

A student copies on his paper the scores of two opposing teams. He writes the numbers as a proper fraction. Then he finds the fraction's simplest form. He repeats the steps until he simplifies ten fractions.

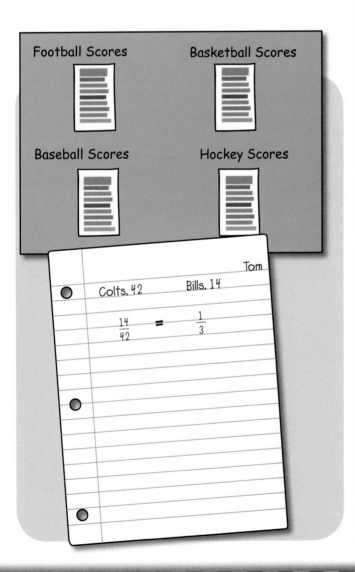

Domino Comparisons

Fractions

Materials:
10 dominoes with at least one pip in each section
paper

A student selects five dominoes and positions them so their pips represent proper fractions. She compares the fraction represented by the first domino to those represented by each remaining domino without repeating any combination. To record her work, she draws each domino pair on her paper and writes the correct symbol between the drawings. She continues until she makes a total of ten different comparisons.

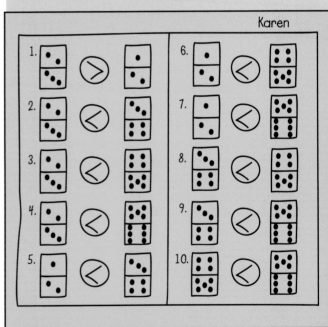

It Makes "Cents"!

Probability

Materials:
play money (coins)
index cards, each labeled with a different
 number of coins and total and with probability
 questions like the ones shown
paper

A student selects a card and writes on her paper the coins needed to equal the amount named in the problem. Then she answers the probability questions based on those coins. She repeats the steps for each card.

Card 2

Find 11 coins that total $0.59.

What is the probability of one of those coins being a...
 quarter?
 dime?
 nickel?
 penny?
 coin that is not a nickel?

Card 1

Find 12 coins that total $0.63.

What is the probability of one of those coins being a...
 quarter?
 dime?
 nickel?
 penny?
 coin that is not a nickel?

Brooke

Card 1
one quarter, three dimes, and eight
pennies
$\frac{1}{12}$
$\frac{3}{12}$, or $\frac{1}{4}$
0
$\frac{8}{12}$, or $\frac{2}{3}$
$\frac{12}{12}$, or 1

Domino Dimensions

Perimeter and area

Materials:
10 dominoes with at least two pips in each section
paper

A student heads his paper as shown. He selects a domino and draws a rectangle (or a square) with dimensions that match the domino's pips. Then he calculates that figure's perimeter and area and records each measurement on his paper. He repeats the steps with each domino.

	Domino	Figure	Perimeter	Area
1.		3 2	10 units	6 square units
2.				

Set 24

Sweet Treat

Fractions

Materials:
copy of the fraction strips from page 98
die
drawing paper

A student rolls the die twice and writes a fraction on his paper, using the smaller number as the numerator and the larger number as the denominator. He repeats the steps until he has five different fractions. Next, he draws a large ice cream cone, divides it into seven parts, and labels the top part "1" and the bottom part "0" as shown. Then, using the fraction strips for help, he copies his fractions in order between the labels.

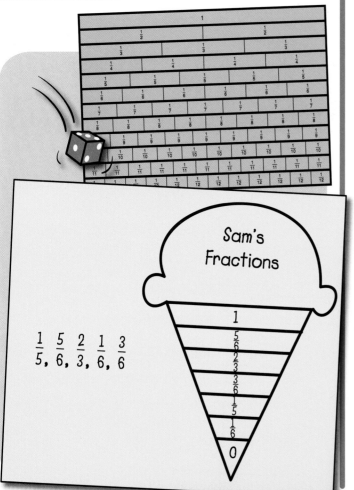

$$\frac{1}{5}, \frac{5}{6}, \frac{2}{3}, \frac{1}{6}, \frac{3}{6}$$

Sam's Fractions

1
$\frac{5}{6}$
$\frac{2}{3}$
$\frac{3}{6}$
$\frac{1}{5}$
$\frac{1}{6}$
0

Order Them!

Mixed numbers

Materials:
copy of the fraction strips from page 98
10 index cards, each labeled with a
    different mixed number
paper

A student uses the fraction strips to help her order the cards from largest to smallest. Then she copies the numbers on her paper.

$9\frac{3}{4}$

$9\frac{2}{5}$

$9\frac{3}{10}$

$8\frac{11}{12}$

$8\frac{7}{8}$

$8\frac{5}{6}$

$7\frac{2}{3}$

$7\frac{3}{5}$

$7\frac{1}{8}$

$6\frac{1}{5}$

Mia

Mixed numbers from
largest to smallest

$9\frac{3}{4}, 9\frac{2}{5}, 9\frac{3}{10}, 8\frac{11}{12}, 8\frac{7}{8}, 8\frac{5}{6}, 7\frac{2}{3},$

$7\frac{3}{5}, 7\frac{1}{8}, 6\frac{1}{5}$

The Space Inside

Volume

Materials:
5 small empty boxes
ruler
paper

> Possible boxes include ones that once contained paper clips, crayons, markers, file folders, and cereal.

A student lists the box types in a chart on his paper. He draws a star by the box he thinks will have the greatest volume. Next, he measures each box, records its dimensions, and finds its volume. Then he circles the box with the greatest volume and compares it to his prediction.

Tyrone

Box	Length	Width	Height	Volume
crayons	9.5 cm	7 cm	2.5 cm	166.25 cm³
markers	14 cm	13 cm	1.5 cm	273 cm³
paper clips	7 cm	4.5 cm	2.5 cm	78.75 cm³
staples	11 cm	5.5 cm	2 cm	121 cm³
brass fasteners	9 cm	6 cm	3 cm	162 cm³

It's a Match!

Algebraic expressions

Materials:
copy of page 99, cut apart
envelope for storing the cards

A student takes the cards from the envelope and puts the answer key aside. She places the cards facedown; then she turns two cards faceup. If the cards match, she sets them aside. If not, she turns them facedown again and turns two more cards faceup. She continues in this manner until she makes all the matches. Then she checks her work against the key.

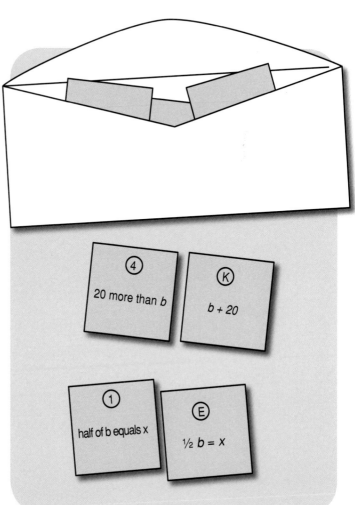

4
20 more than b

K
b + 20

1
half of b equals x

E
½ b = x

Attribute Sort

Fractions

Materials:
3 clear plastic bags numbered 1–3, each filled
  with attribute blocks representing every
  attribute in the list shown
12 index cards, each labeled with a different
  attribute from the list
paper

A student selects a card and writes on his paper a
fraction that tells what part of the blocks in each bag
represents the attribute on the card. He then writes
the three fractions from the least to the greatest. He
repeats the steps four more times, using a different
attribute card each time.

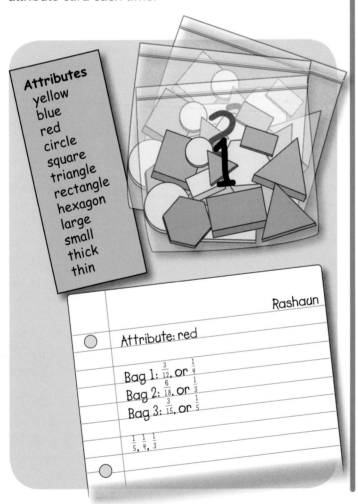

Attributes
yellow
blue
red
circle
square
triangle
rectangle
hexagon
large
small
thick
thin

Rashaun

Attribute: red

Bag 1: $\frac{3}{12}$ or $\frac{1}{4}$
Bag 2: $\frac{6}{18}$ or $\frac{1}{3}$
Bag 3: $\frac{3}{15}$ or $\frac{1}{5}$

$\frac{1}{5}$, $\frac{1}{4}$, $\frac{1}{3}$

Domino Draw

Fractions

Materials:
10 dominoes with one or more pips in each section
paper

A student selects a domino and positions it so that
its pips represent an improper fraction. She draws the
domino on her paper and writes the corresponding
fraction next to the drawing. Then she converts the
fraction to a mixed or whole number. She repeats the
steps, using a different domino each time, until she
converts ten fractions.

	Domino	Fraction	Mixed Number or Whole Number
1.		$\frac{5}{2}$	$2\frac{1}{2}$
2.		$\frac{4}{3}$	$1\frac{1}{3}$
3.		$\frac{6}{5}$	$1\frac{1}{5}$
4.		$\frac{5}{3}$	$1\frac{2}{3}$
5.		$\frac{6}{3}$	2
6.		$\frac{3}{2}$	$1\frac{1}{2}$
7.		$\frac{6}{2}$	3
8.		$\frac{5}{4}$	$1\frac{1}{4}$
9.		$\frac{3}{3}$	1
10.		$\frac{6}{1}$	6

All Wrapped Up?

Surface area

Materials:
3 empty boxes
index card labeled as shown
ruler
paper

Possible boxes include ones that contained paper clips, crayons, tissues, shoes, cereal, or crackers.

A student selects a box and measures the length and width of each side to the nearest half inch. He calculates the area of each side, records the measurements in a chart on his paper, and finds the surface area by adding the six numbers together. Then he compares the sum to the amount of gift wrap on the card to determine whether there is enough gift wrap to cover the box.

gift wrap = 196 square inches

| Box | Area of Each Side | | | | | | Surface Area | Enough Wrapping Paper? |
	1	2	3	4	5	6		
tissue	20.25 sq. in.	22.5 sq. in.	22.5 sq. in.	22.5 sq. in.	22.5 sq. in.	20.25 sq. in.	130.5 sq. in.	yes

Slides, Flips, and Turns

Transformations

Materials:
tagboard alphabet (or number) cutouts
3 markers (red, blue, and yellow)
index card labeled as shown
paper

A student selects a cutout and traces it on her paper. Next, she slides, flips, or turns the cutout and traces it in its new position. She then numbers the new tracing "1" and colors it according to the code. She continues sliding, flipping, or turning the cutout from each new tracing, coloring and numbering each appropriately, until she has ten colorful numbered tracings.

Color Code

translation=yellow
rotation = blue
reflection = red

Take Your Positions!

Fractions

Materials:
12 dominoes with one or more pips in each section
paper

A student selects three dominoes and positions them vertically to represent three proper fractions. He arranges the dominoes so that the fractions they represent are ordered from greatest to least. Then he writes the fractions on his paper. He repeats the steps until he has used all the dominoes and recorded four sets of fractions.

Mark

Set 1: $\frac{3}{5}$, $\frac{1}{2}$, $\frac{2}{6}$

Time to Think

Fractions

Materials:
index cards, each labeled with a word problem like the ones shown
paper

A student reads each problem, writes her estimate on her paper, and then explains her thinking. She continues until she has estimated answers to all the problems.

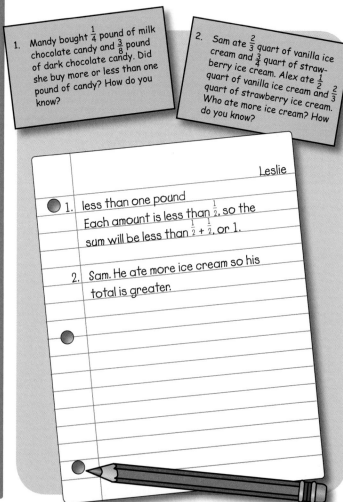

1. Mandy bought $\frac{1}{4}$ pound of milk chocolate candy and $\frac{3}{8}$ pound of dark chocolate candy. Did she buy more or less than one pound of candy? How do you know?

2. Sam ate $\frac{2}{3}$ quart of vanilla ice cream and $\frac{3}{4}$ quart of strawberry ice cream. Alex ate $\frac{1}{2}$ quart of vanilla ice cream and $\frac{2}{3}$ quart of strawberry ice cream. Who ate more ice cream? How do you know?

Leslie

1. less than one pound
Each amount is less than $\frac{1}{2}$, so the sum will be less than $\frac{1}{2} + \frac{1}{2}$, or 1.

2. Sam. He ate more ice cream so his total is greater.

Same Amount

Weight

Materials:
pairs of index cards, each pair labeled in red
   and blue with matching weights similar
   to the pair shown (see also the student paper)
paper

A student shuffles the cards and arranges them faceup in rows. He matches a card labeled in red with one labeled in blue that shows an equal amount. He continues in this manner until all cards are paired. Then he writes the matching amounts on his paper.

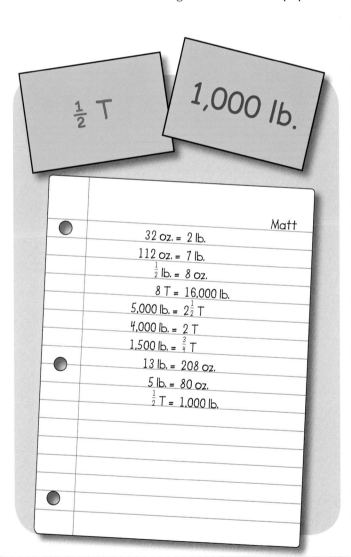

Matt

32 oz. = 2 lb.
112 oz. = 7 lb.
$\frac{1}{2}$ lb. = 8 oz.
8 T = 16,000 lb.
5,000 lb. = $2\frac{1}{2}$ T
4,000 lb. = 2 T
1,500 lb. = $\frac{3}{4}$ T
13 lb. = 208 oz.
5 lb. = 80 oz.
$\frac{1}{2}$ T = 1,000 lb.

Meteorological Math

Mean, median, mode, and range

Materials:
index cards, each labeled with a different set
   of temperatures as shown
paper

A student calculates the mean, median, mode, and range of City A's temperatures and writes her answers on her paper. She then repeats the steps for City B and City C.

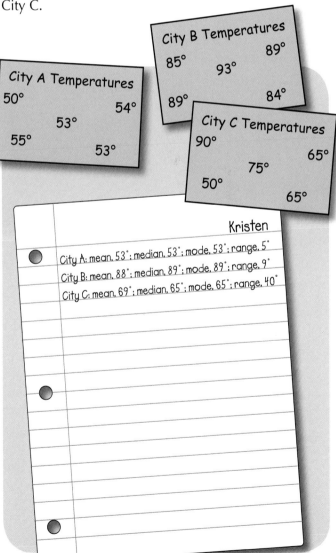

Kristen

City A: mean, 53°; median, 53°; mode, 53°; range, 5°
City B: mean, 88°; median, 89°; mode, 89°; range, 9°
City C: mean, 69°; median, 65°; mode, 65°; range, 40°

Let's Change Forms!

Relating fractions and decimals

Materials:
index cards, each numbered and labeled
    with a fraction or decimal
base ten blocks
paper

A student selects an index card and uses base ten blocks to model the number on the card. She uses flats to represent whole numbers, rods for tenths, and units for hundredths. Then she draws the model on her paper and writes the fraction and decimal equivalents. She repeats the process with each remaining card.

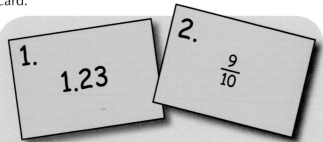

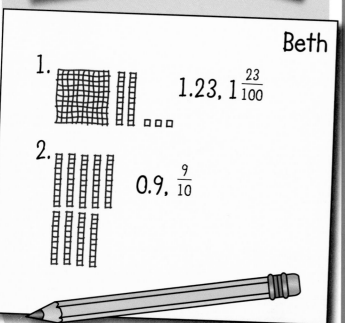

Order Up!

Fractions

Materials:
student copies of the single quadrant grid on page 100
construction paper (one sheet per child)
colored pencils
glue

A student glues a grid to a sheet of construction paper and chooses a colored pencil. He programs the grid with two sets of ordered pairs, making sure the first number in each pair is less than the second. Using the *x*-coordinates as numerators and the *y*-coordinates as denominators, he writes an addition problem below the grid and solves it. He repeats the steps using different-colored pencils and ordered pairs until he has solved three addition problems in all.

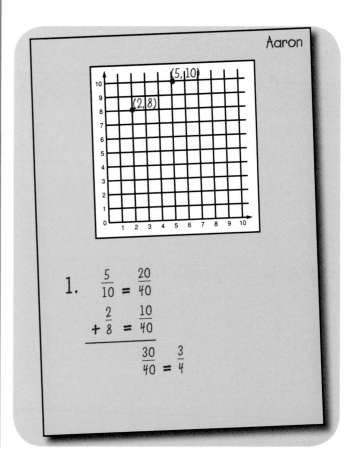

Day of Your Dreams

Elapsed time

Materials:
student copies of the form on page 100

A student decides what she would do in one day if she could do anything she wanted. She lists each activity and its start and stop times on a copy of the form. Then she calculates the length of time she will do each activity and records it on her form.

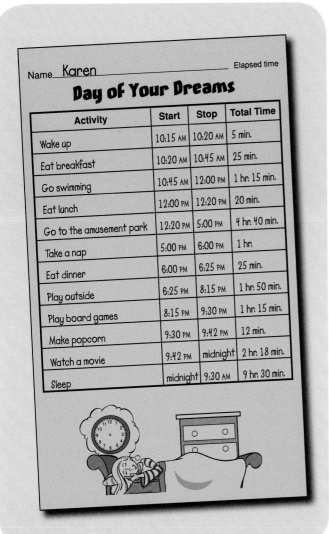

Name **Karen**   Elapsed time

Day of Your Dreams

Activity	Start	Stop	Total Time
Wake up	10:15 AM	10:20 AM	5 min.
Eat breakfast	10:20 AM	10:45 AM	25 min.
Go swimming	10:45 AM	12:00 PM	1 hr. 15 min.
Eat lunch	12:00 PM	12:20 PM	20 min.
Go to the amusement park	12:20 PM	5:00 PM	4 hr. 40 min.
Take a nap	5:00 PM	6:00 PM	1 hr.
Eat dinner	6:00 PM	6:25 PM	25 min.
Play outside	6:25 PM	8:15 PM	1 hr. 50 min.
Play board games	8:15 PM	9:30 PM	1 hr. 15 min.
Make popcorn	9:30 PM	9:42 PM	12 min.
Watch a movie	9:42 PM	midnight	2 hr. 18 min.
Sleep	midnight	9:30 AM	9 hr. 30 min.

Pattern Poster

Number patterns

Materials:
list of number patterns, like the one shown
light-colored construction paper
markers

A student selects a number pattern from the list and writes the pattern's name across the top of his paper. He illustrates the pattern. Then he writes a brief paragraph to explain his illustration.

Number Patterns

dividing with zeros
multiplying with zeros
powers of ten
squared numbers
triangular numbers

Tim

Triangular Numbers

1   3   6   10   15   21   28   36   45
+2 +3 +4 +5 +6 +7 +8 +9

Triangular numbers are formed by adding consecutive numbers. For example, 0 + 1 = 1, 1 + 2 = 3, 3 + 3 = 6, 6 + 4 = 10, and so on. To show the first nine triangular numbers, I drew dots so they formed triangles.

Roll With It!

Fractions

Materials:
student copies of the cube pattern on page 98
timer
scissors
tape
paper

A student programs each side of a cube cutout with a fraction and then assembles the cube. Next, he sets the timer for ten minutes and rolls the cube twice, recording on his paper each fraction rolled. Then he adds or subtracts the two fractions. He continues to create and solve problems in this manner until his time is up.

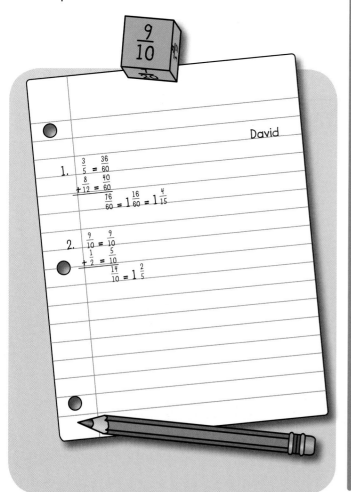

The Answer Is ...

Fractions

Materials:
5 envelopes labeled A–E, each containing
    3 to 5 fraction cards that when added
    together equal 1 as shown
paper

A student takes one fraction card from envelope A. On her paper, she subtracts the fraction from 1. Then she takes a second card from the envelope and subtracts that fraction from her answer. She continues in this manner until there are no more cards in the envelope. If her final answer is zero, she repeats the steps with the next envelope. If her final answer is not zero, she subtracts the same fractions again.

Fractions That Equal 1 When Added Together
$\frac{1}{6} + \frac{1}{3} + \frac{1}{2}$
$\frac{1}{3} + \frac{2}{5} + \frac{4}{15}$
$\frac{1}{4} + \frac{3}{8} + \frac{1}{3} + \frac{1}{24}$
$\frac{3}{4} + \frac{1}{6} + \frac{1}{12}$
$\frac{2}{5} + \frac{1}{10} + \frac{1}{3} + \frac{1}{6}$
$\frac{1}{3} + \frac{1}{4} + \frac{1}{5} + \frac{1}{6} + \frac{1}{20}$

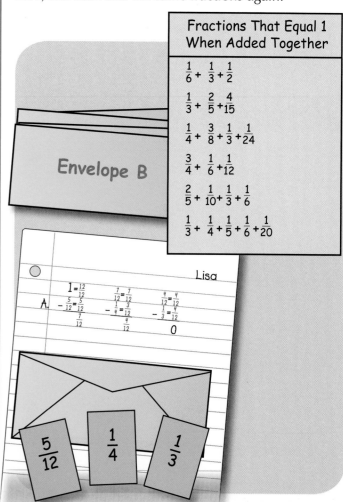

Garden Time

Area and perimeter

Materials:
graph paper (one sheet per child)
construction paper (one sheet per child)
colored pencils
scissors
glue

A student cuts a rectangle (garden) from the graph paper, glues it to construction paper, and creates a color code for four vegetables of her choice. She "plants" her vegetables in different sections of her garden by coloring squares on the grid according to the code. Then, with each side of each square equal to one foot, she finds the perimeter and area of her entire garden and of each garden section, and records the measurements on her paper.

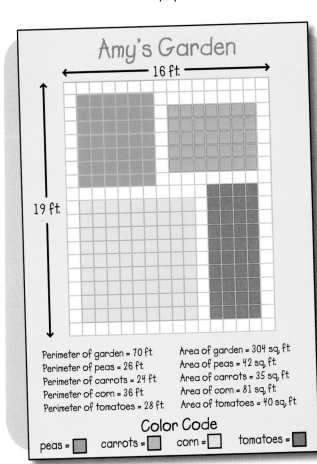

Amy's Garden

← 16 ft. →

19 ft.

Perimeter of garden = 70 ft.   Area of garden = 304 sq. ft.
Perimeter of peas = 26 ft.   Area of peas = 42 sq. ft.
Perimeter of carrots = 24 ft.   Area of carrots = 35 sq. ft.
Perimeter of corn = 36 ft.   Area of corn = 81 sq. ft.
Perimeter of tomatoes = 28 ft.   Area of tomatoes = 40 sq. ft.

Color Code
peas = ▢   carrots = ▢   corn = ▢   tomatoes = ▢

Take Your Pick

Solid figures

Materials:
play dough
toothpicks
timer
colored pencils
paper

A student sets the timer for 15 minutes. He uses the play dough and toothpicks to create a cube, prism, or pyramid. On his paper, he draws a picture of his shape and labels it. Then he disassembles his shape and builds a different one. He repeats the steps until time is up.

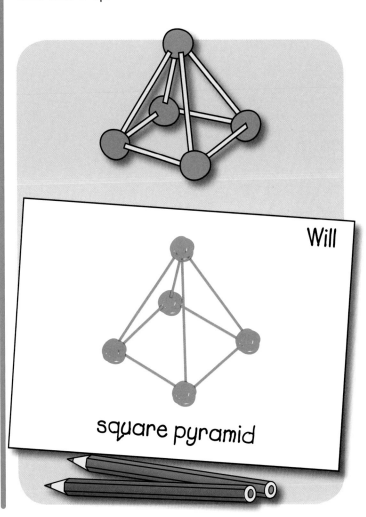

Will

square pyramid

Presidential Birthdays

Fractions

Materials:
student copies of page 101
paper

A student completes a copy of page 101 by writing each president's birthday as a fraction, using the month as the numerator and the day as the denominator. Next, she uses the presidents' names to write on her paper ten addition problems. Then she solves each problem and writes the answer in simplest form.

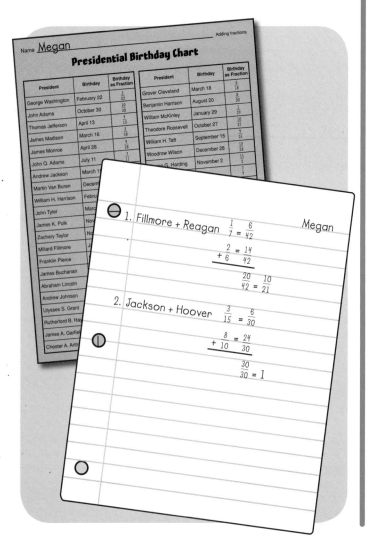

Flower Power

Fractions

For partners

Materials:
student copies of page 102
construction paper (one sheet per student)
scissors
tape
paper

Each student cuts out his patterns, makes six colorful petals by tracing the single petal onto construction paper, and cuts out the tracings. He programs the petal cutouts with three addition and three subtraction problems (one problem on each petal) and writes each answer on a different petal of his flower cutout. Next, the partners trade cutouts and solve the problems on paper. The students then place each petal cutout atop its matching answer and tape the outer edges together to create liftable flaps.

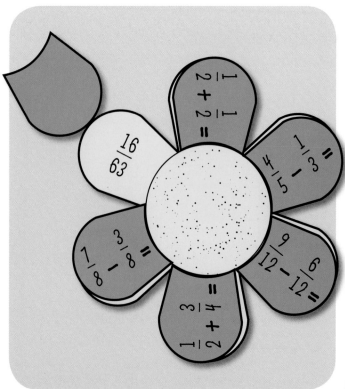

Pick a Card

Angles

Materials:
small paper bag filled with 10 index cards
    labeled with measurements as shown
protractor
paper

    A student draws three cards from the bag. She writes the measurements on her paper as an addition problem, finds the sum, and puts the cards back in the bag. Then she uses a protractor to draw on her paper an angle of that size. She repeats the steps until she has constructed three different angles.

Cube Soup

Probability

Materials:
3 labeled bowls, each filled with a different
    number of Unifix cubes in several colors
index card labeled with five probability questions
    like the one shown
paper

    A student selects a bowl. He reads the questions on the index card. Next, he sorts the cubes by color, writes on his paper an answer for each question, and returns the cubes to the bowl. He repeats the steps with each remaining bowl.

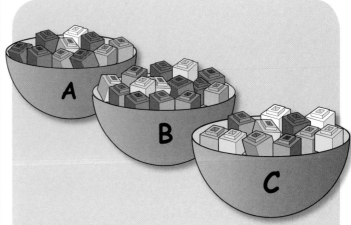

Question Card

1. What is the probability of getting a red cube?
2. What is the probability of not getting a green cube?
3. What is the probability of getting a cube that is blue or yellow?
4. What is the probability of not getting a black cube?
5. What is the probability of getting a cube that is orange, brown, or maroon?

Planting Time

Problem solving

Materials:
copy of page 103
index cards (three per student)

A student uses the information on the seed packets to write three word problems. She writes each problem on the front of an index card and its answer on the back.

Pam wants to plant one row of flowers. She wants to plant two morning glories, five bachelor buttons, and six zinnias. About how long will her row of flowers be?

Sort the Sums

Mixed numbers

Materials:
3 paper plates labeled as shown
12 index cards labeled with problems such as those shown paper

A student selects a problem, solves it on his paper, and writes the fraction in its simplest form. Then he uses his answer to sort the card onto the correct plate. He continues in this manner until he solves all the problems and sorts all the cards.

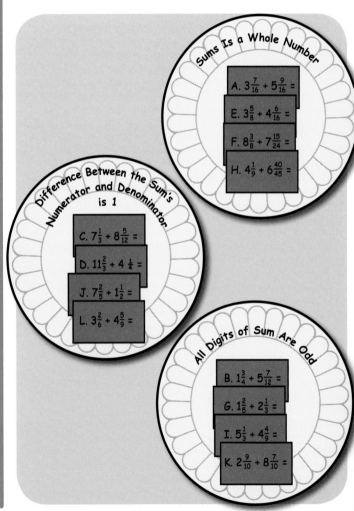

Sums Is a Whole Number

A. $3\frac{7}{16} + 5\frac{9}{16} =$

E. $3\frac{5}{8} + 4\frac{6}{16} =$

F. $8\frac{3}{8} + 7\frac{15}{24} =$

H. $4\frac{1}{9} + 6\frac{40}{45} =$

Difference Between the Sum's Numerator and Denominator is 1

C. $7\frac{1}{3} + 8\frac{5}{12} =$

D. $11\frac{2}{3} + 4\frac{1}{4} =$

J. $7\frac{2}{5} + 1\frac{1}{2} =$

L. $3\frac{2}{6} + 4\frac{5}{9} =$

All Digits of Sum Are Odd

B. $1\frac{3}{4} + 5\frac{7}{12} =$

G. $1\frac{2}{5} + 2\frac{1}{3} =$

I. $5\frac{1}{3} + 4\frac{4}{9} =$

K. $2\frac{9}{10} + 8\frac{7}{10} =$

Map It!

Linear measurement

Materials:
state road map
construction paper (one sheet per student)
yarn or string
scissors
glue
ruler

A student locates his town on the map and also selects a place he would like to visit. He writes on his paper detailed directions telling how to reach that destination from his town. Next, he marks the route on the map with yarn, cuts a short piece of yarn equal to that distance, and glues it to his paper. Then he measures the yarn's length with the ruler, uses the map's scale to find the approximate distance the length represents, and records the data on his paper.

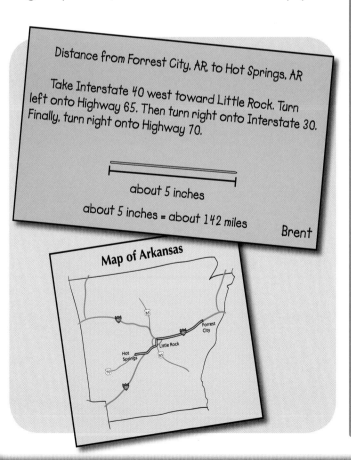

Distance from Forrest City, AR, to Hot Springs, AR

Take Interstate 40 west toward Little Rock. Turn left onto Highway 65. Then turn right onto Interstate 30. Finally, turn right onto Highway 70.

about 5 inches

about 5 inches = about 142 miles

Brent

Map of Arkansas

Make an Ice Pop!

Variables and inequalities

Materials:
10 craft sticks, each labeled with a different
    solution from the list
10 index cards, each labeled as shown with
    a different problem from the list
large envelope for storing the craft sticks
    and index cards
paper

A student removes the craft sticks and index cards from the envelope. Next, she lists on her paper for each card all possible answers for *n*. She then pairs each ice pop with an ice pop stick, making sure that all the numbers on the stick work for that particular equation or expression.

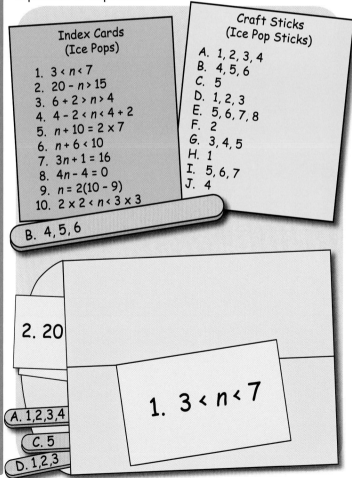

Index Cards
(Ice Pops)

1. $3 < n < 7$
2. $20 - n > 15$
3. $6 + 2 > n > 4$
4. $4 - 2 < n < 4 + 2$
5. $n + 10 = 2 \times 7$
6. $n + 6 < 10$
7. $3n + 1 = 16$
8. $4n - 4 = 0$
9. $n = 2(10 - 9)$
10. $2 \times 2 < n < 3 \times 3$

Craft Sticks
(Ice Pop Sticks)

A. 1, 2, 3, 4
B. 4, 5, 6
C. 5
D. 1, 2, 3
E. 5, 6, 7, 8
F. 2
G. 3, 4, 5
H. 1
I. 5, 6, 7
J. 4

B. 4, 5, 6

2. 20

1. $3 < n < 7$

A. 1,2,3,4

C. 5

D. 1,2,3

Stick With It!

Mixed numbers

Materials:
10 craft sticks labeled as shown
2 plastic cups labeled as shown
paper

A student selects a craft stick and solves its problem on her paper. She places the stick in the corresponding cup and then repeats the process with the remaining craft sticks.

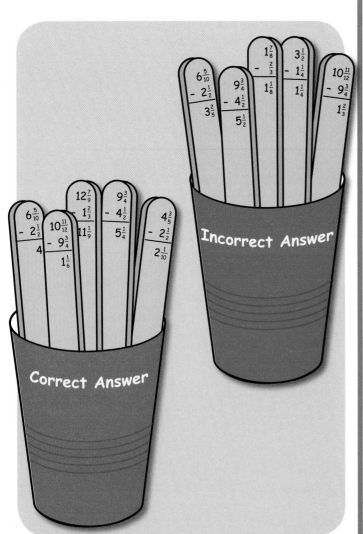

Recipe Revisions

Mixed numbers

Materials:
student copies of page 104
paper

A student reads the top recipe card. She pretends that she must use the recipe to make enough cookies for 250 people. Based on the number of cookies the given recipe makes, she determines the number by which she must multiply the amount of each ingredient. She calculates the new measurements on her paper and then writes the numbers on the bottom recipe card.

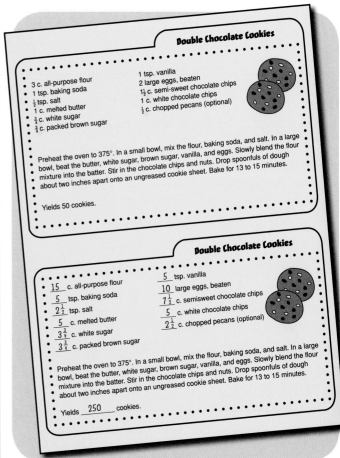

I Spy

Volume

Materials:
half sheets of construction paper (one per student)
scissors
ruler

A student folds her construction paper in half and cuts five flaps in the top sheet as shown. She selects five classroom objects and writes each object's name on a different flap. Next, she measures each object and records its measurements on the back of its flap. Then she calculates the object's volume and records it under the corresponding flap. She continues until she has recorded the volume of all five objects.

in. x 3 in. x 2.5 in. = 22.5 in.^{3}

.75 in. x 3.75 in. x 1 in. = 10.3125 in.^{3}

tissue box

$V = 22.5$ in.^{3}

$V = 10.3125$ in.^{3}

pack of notebook paper

pencil box

Net Worth

Solid figures

Materials:
student copies of pages 105–107 and the cube
    pattern from page 98
colored pencils
scissors
tape

A student writes the name of each net on the line provided. On one face of each net, he draws, colors, and labels an everyday object that is an example of the solid the unassembled net represents. On each remaining face or base, he writes an attribute of that solid. Then he cuts out each net and assembles it using tape.

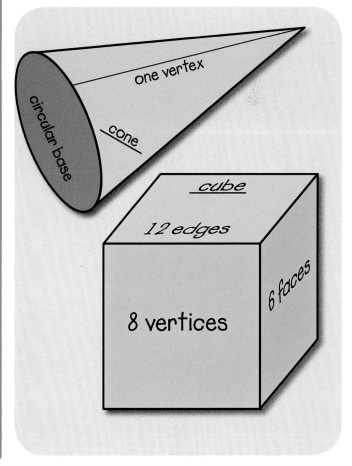

one vertex

circular base

cone

cube

12 edges

6 faces

8 vertices

It's in the Bag!

Multiplication

For partners

Materials:
student copies of page 108
2 paper lunch bags labeled as shown
10 dominoes (no blanks) in each bag

A student pulls a domino from the fraction bag. Both students record the domino as a fraction on their recording sheets. Next, the other partner pulls a domino from the whole number bag and both students record the domino as a whole number. Each partner then solves the problem, racing to see who finds the product faster. The winner pulls the next two dominoes from the bags. Play continues in this manner until all the dominoes have been used.

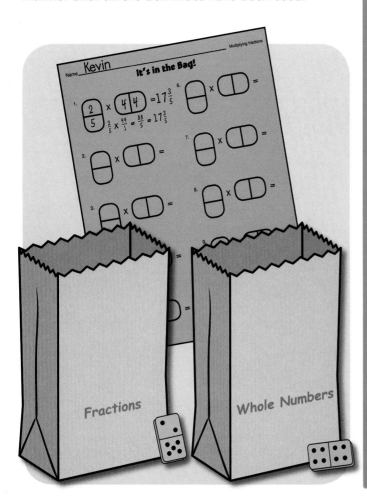

Shake, Rattle, and Roll

Fractions

Materials:
clear plastic bottle with 2 dice inside
timer
paper

A student sets the timer for five minutes. Next, she shakes the bottle and forms a fraction with the two numbers rolled. She shakes the bottle again to form a second fraction. The student then finds the product of the two fractions. She repeats this process until time runs out.

Flat as a Pancake

Surface area

Materials:
3 or 4 small boxes opened flat with tabs removed
and faces labeled, like the ones shown
construction paper (one sheet per child)
ruler

Possible boxes include those for paper clips, staples,
crayons, and markers.

A student selects a box, traces it on her construction paper, and labels the faces. Using a ruler, she measures the length and width of each face and records the measurements below her drawing. She calculates the area of each face and then finds the sum of the areas.

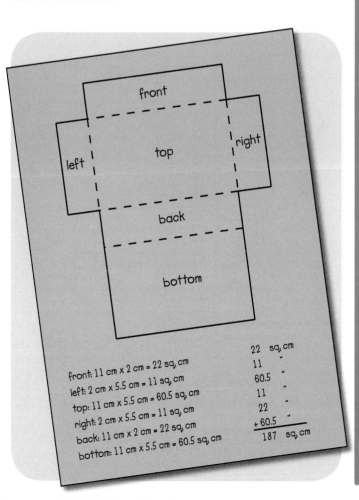

front: 11 cm x 2 cm = 22 sq. cm   22 sq. cm
left: 2 cm x 5.5 cm = 11 sq. cm   11 "
top: 11 cm x 5.5 cm = 60.5 sq. cm   60.5 "
right: 2 cm x 5.5 cm = 11 sq. cm   11 "
back: 11 cm x 2 cm = 22 sq. cm   22 "
bottom: 11 cm x 5.5 cm = 60.5 sq. cm + 60.5 "
                                      187 sq. cm

In the News

Graphs

Materials:
newspapers and magazines
construction paper (one sheet per student)
scissors
glue

A student cuts a graph from a newspaper or magazine and glues it to his construction paper. Below the graph, he writes five to ten questions that can be answered by looking at the graph. He answers the questions on the back of his paper.

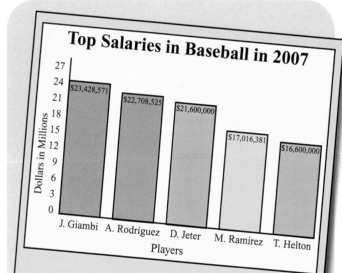

1. What is the salary range of these players?
2. What is the median?
3. What is the mean?
4. How much more money does Giambi make than Jeter?
5. Which player makes about $700,000 less than Giambi?
6. Which player makes five million dollars more than Helton?

Bottle Tops

Fractions

Materials:
student copies of page 109
colored pencils
paper

A student multiplies on his paper two fractions from gameboard A: one from the top row by one from the left column. He records the product in the circle where the row and column intersect. Then he colors the matching fraction in the answer bank. He continues in this manner until all the circles on both gameboards are filled in.

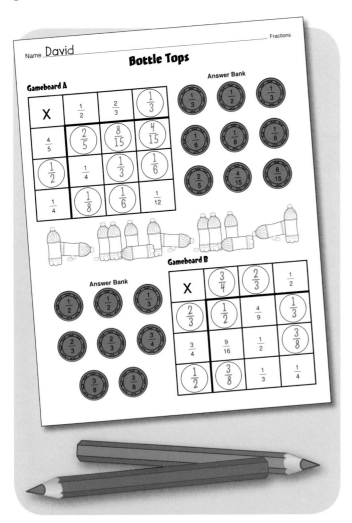

On a Roll!

Mixed numbers

Materials:
copies of the cube pattern from page 98 (three per student)
scissors
tape
paper

A student labels the faces of one pattern with two plus signs, two minus signs, and two multiplication signs. She labels each face of a second and a third pattern with a different mixed number. Next, she cuts out the patterns and assembles the cubes. Then she rolls all three cubes, and depending on the operation sign rolled, she adds, subtracts, or multiplies on her paper the two mixed numbers rolled. She continues solving problems in this manner until there are no new combinations.

That's the Angle!

Angles

For partners

Materials:
2 rulers
2 protractors
paper

Each student draws on his paper an angle and estimates its measurement. Next, he measures the angle with a protractor and records the actual measurement on his paper, giving himself one point for each degree that his guess differs from the actual measurement. He then draws, estimates, and measures four more angles in the same manner. The partner with fewer points wins.

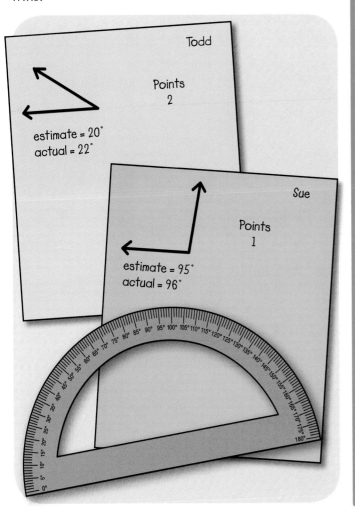

Substitution

Algebraic expressions

Materials:
4 index cards labeled as shown
die
paper

A student selects a card. She copies on her paper the card's expression and then numbers the next three lines from 1 to 3. Next, she rolls the die and records on line 1 the number rolled. She continues rolling the die until she has recorded three different numbers on lines 1–3. The student solves the expression by substituting each of the recorded numbers for the variable. She repeats the steps for each remaining expression.

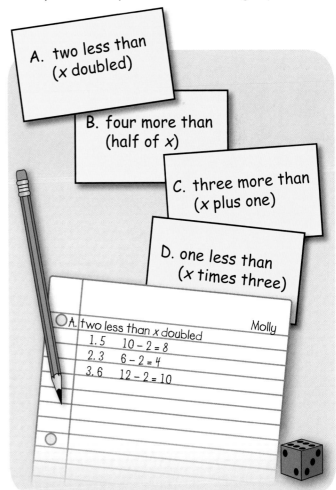

Color-Coded Products

Fractions

Materials:
5 crayons (red, green, blue, orange, and yellow)
paper

A student draws a 6 x 2 grid on her paper. In four of her grid's boxes, she colors a red square. Then she colors a green square in three boxes, a blue square in two boxes, an orange square in two boxes, and a yellow square in one box. Next, she makes a chart to show how much of her total grid each color represents. Then she uses the colors and the fractions they represent to write and solve ten different multiplication problems.

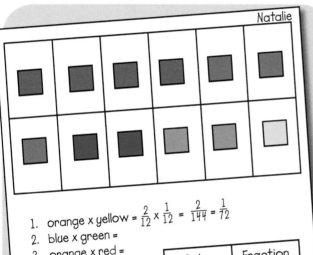

Natalie

1. orange x yellow = $\frac{2}{12} \times \frac{1}{12} = \frac{2}{144} = \frac{1}{72}$
2. blue x green =
3. orange x red =
4. red x yellow =
5. red x blue =
6. green x yellow =
7. orange x green =
8. red x green =
9. blue x orange =
10. blue x yellow =

Color	Fraction
red	$\frac{4}{12}$, or $\frac{1}{3}$
green	$\frac{3}{12}$, or $\frac{1}{4}$
blue	$\frac{2}{12}$, or $\frac{1}{6}$
orange	$\frac{2}{12}$, or $\frac{1}{6}$
yellow	$\frac{1}{12}$

All Decked Out

Fractions

Materials:
deck of cards (without face cards)
cube pattern from page 98 programmed with
    basic operations and assembled
paper

A student stacks the deck of cards facedown and draws four cards. He uses the cards' numbers to create any two fractions and records them on his paper. Next, he rolls the die to determine which operation he will perform with the fractions. He continues to write and solve problems in this manner until there are no more cards in the deck.

1. $\frac{7}{9} \times \frac{2}{10} = \frac{14}{90} = \frac{7}{45}$

Jacob

multiply
subtract

Fill 'er Up!

Volume

Materials:
gram unit cubes
student copies of page 105 and the cube pattern
    from page 98
scissors
tape

A student cuts out the nets and assembles them, leaving one side open. She then estimates how many gram unit cubes will fill each shape and writes her guess on one face of each shape. Next, she fills each shape with cubes and writes the actual count on another face of the shape. Then she removes the cubes and finishes assembling the shapes.

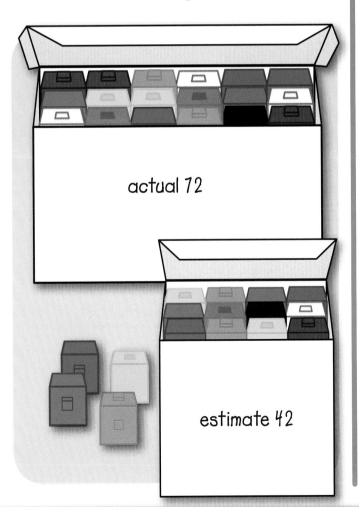

actual 72

estimate 42

Picture Perfect

Geometry

Materials:
magazines
permanent marker
glue
paper
scissors

A student cuts out a picture from a magazine and glues it to his paper. Using the marker, he circles or marks on the picture ten different examples of geometric concepts and then draws an arrow to and numbers each one. On the back of his paper, he identifies the concept to which each arrow points.

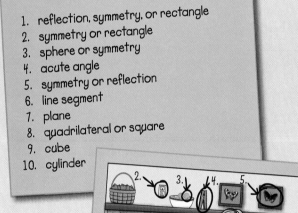

1. reflection, symmetry, or rectangle
2. symmetry or rectangle
3. sphere or symmetry
4. acute angle
5. symmetry or reflection
6. line segment
7. plane
8. quadrilateral or square
9. cube
10. cylinder

Brad

Time to Match

Fractions and percents

Materials:
timer
20 index card halves labeled with fractions
20 index card halves labeled with matching percents

A student shuffles the cards, places them face-down, and sets the timer for five minutes. Then she turns over two cards. If the cards are a matching fraction and percent, she sets the cards aside. If not, she turns them facedown again and turns over two more cards. She makes as many matches as possible before the time is up.

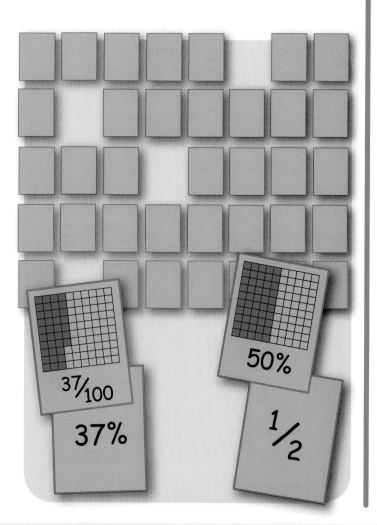

Graphic Math

Fractions, decimals, and percents

Materials:
student copies of the 10 x 10 grid on page 110
crayons
scissors
glue
paper

A student colors squares on a grid to create a picture. Next, he cuts out his grid and glues it to his paper. Below the grid, he creates a color key. Then he writes a fraction, a decimal, and a percent to represent each amount of color in the picture.

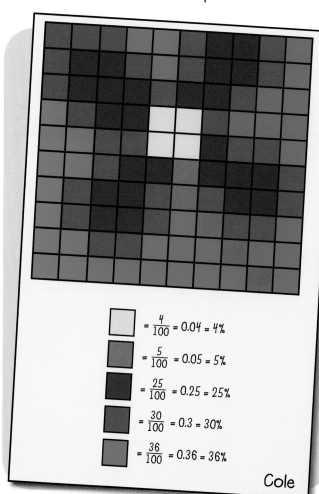

$= \frac{4}{100} = 0.04 = 4\%$

$= \frac{5}{100} = 0.05 = 5\%$

$= \frac{25}{100} = 0.25 = 25\%$

$= \frac{30}{100} = 0.3 = 30\%$

$= \frac{36}{100} = 0.36 = 36\%$

Cole

A Box Bonanza

Surface area

Materials:
small boxes, opened flat with tabs removed
    and faces labeled
student copies of centimeter graph paper
construction paper (one sheet per student)
ruler
scissors
glue

Possible boxes include a crayon box, a tissue box, a staple box, and a paper clip box.

A student selects a box and records on her paper the length and width of each of its faces. She calculates each face's area and then finds the sum of the areas. Next, she traces the selected box on graph paper and labels its sections. Then she cuts out the tracing and glues it to her paper. Finally, she counts the sections' squares and compares them to the total area she calculated.

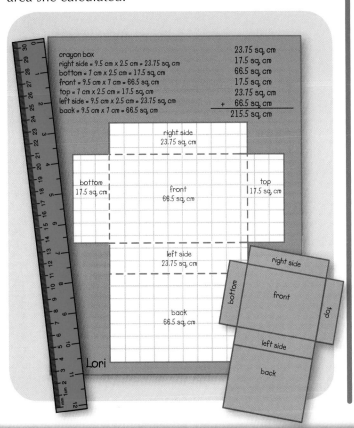

Sensational School Day

Circle graphs

Materials:
paper plates (one per student)
ruler
colored pencils
paper

A student pretends that he gets to plan his dream day at school. On his paper, he lists each activity he would like to do and how long he wants it to last, making sure the total time equals the length of one school day. Then he divides a paper plate into sections (one for each part of the school day) and creates a circle graph to represent his plan.

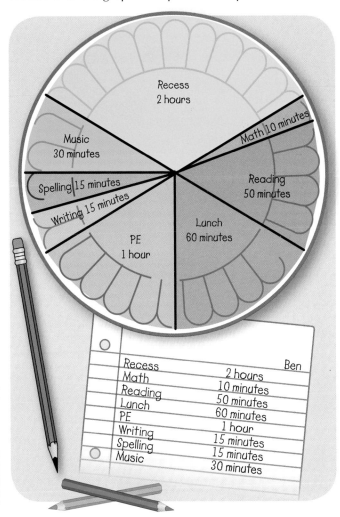

The Flip Side

Percent

Materials:
small bag filled with 20 two-color counters
paper

A student empties the bag and spreads out the counters. She writes on her paper a fraction to show what part of all the counters is red and a fraction to show what part is yellow. She changes each fraction to a percent and then returns the counters to the bag. She repeats the steps as time allows.

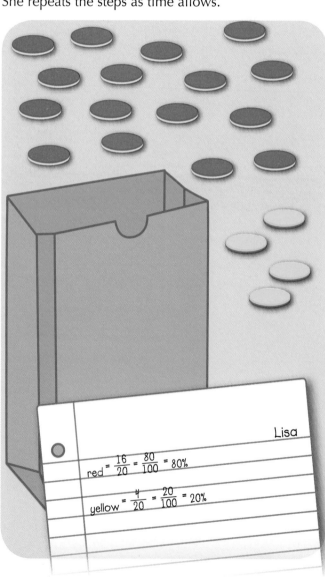

Lisa

$$\text{red} = \frac{16}{20} = \frac{80}{100} = 80\%$$

$$\text{yellow} = \frac{4}{20} = \frac{20}{100} = 20\%$$

It's on the Map!

Fractions, decimals, and percents

Materials:
large U.S. map
small bag filled with small place markers
paper

Possible place markers include small bits of paper, centimeter cubes, and dried beans.

A student randomly sprinkles on the map a handful of markers. On his paper, he writes a fraction showing what part of the 50 states is covered with markers. Then he changes the fraction to a decimal and a percent. He returns the place markers to the bag and repeats the steps until he has converted ten different fractions to decimals.

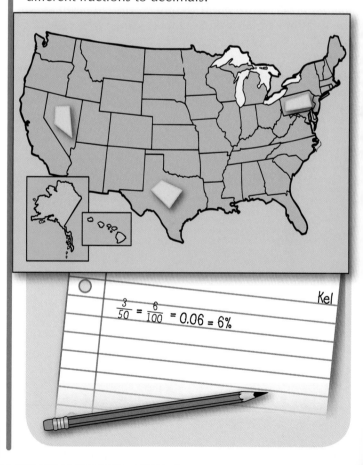

Kel

$$\frac{3}{50} = \frac{6}{100} = 0.06 = 6\%$$

Just Right

Temperature

For partners

Materials:
student copies of the thermometer from page 110
bonus points chart similar to the one shown
two dice
markers in two different colors
paper

Each student selects a marker. One student rolls the dice, records the sum as her points, and colors on a copy of the thermometer a number of degrees equal to her points. Then her partner takes a turn, adding to the degrees colored on the thermometer. If the coloring stops on water's freezing or boiling point, the student receives bonus points according to the chart. Students continue taking turns until one partner's coloring reaches the highest temperature on the thermometer without going over. The partner with more points wins.

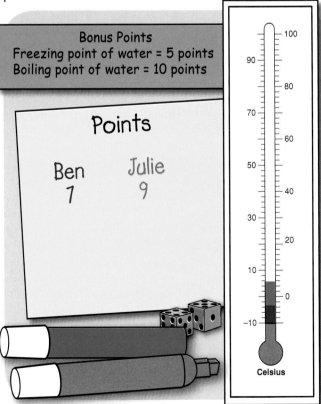

Bonus Points
Freezing point of water = 5 points
Boiling point of water = 10 points

Points

Ben	Julie
7	9

Celsius

What's the Rule?

Input-output tables

Materials:
student copies of the input-output tables from page 110

A student determines the rule for each table, writes the rule in the space provided, and fills in the missing numbers. On the back of her paper, she creates a new table, writes its rule, and fills in its numbers.

Input	Output
0	8
1	9
5	13
9	17

Rule: Add 8.

Input	Output
16	$11\frac{1}{2}$
24	$19\frac{1}{2}$
29	$24\frac{1}{2}$
64	$59\frac{1}{2}$

Rule: Subtract $4\frac{1}{2}$.

Input	Output
18	36
10.5	21
13.5	27
10	20

Rule: Multiply by 2.

Input	Output
20	2
500	50
80	8
100	10

Rule: Divide by 10.

Input	Output
3	15
12.5	62.5
5	25
75	375

Rule: Multiply by 5.

Molly

Number Clues

Use with "Ten Cups" on page 4.

Mystery Number Clues

1. The digit with no value is in the ones place.

2. The tens digit is an odd number. The tenths digit is an even number. Both numbers are multiples of three.

3. The thousandths digit is an even prime number.

4. The largest digit is in the tens place.

5. The hundredths digit is twice the thousandths digit.

6. The millions digit is one less than the tens digit.

7. The thousands digit is an odd number that is one more than the ones digit.

8. The hundred thousands digit is two more than five.

9. The product of the ten thousands digit and the digit to its left is 21.

10. The hundreds digit is a factor of 25 that is greater than 2.

TEC61157

Recording Sheet

Use with "Roll and Write!" on page 4.

Name _____

Roll and Write!

Recording sheet

Number Rolled	Place Value(s) to Represent	Sample Number
	thousands	
	tens	
	hundred thousands	
	hundreds	
	ten thousands	
	ones	
	millions and ones	
	hundred thousands and hundreds	
	thousands, hundreds, and tens	
	millions, ten thousands, and tens	

Super Simple Independent Practice: Math • ©The Mailbox® Books • TEC61157

76

1.261 TEC61157	**13.444** TEC61157	**8.867** TEC61157
4.654 TEC61157	**8.878** TEC61157	**15.030** TEC61157
4.332 TEC61157	**11.716** TEC61157	**9.575** TEC61157
0.223 TEC61157	**5.445** TEC61157	**11.084** TEC61157
8.496 TEC61157	**2.639** TEC61157	**25.011** TEC61157
3.334 TEC61157	**13.173** TEC61157	**14.556** TEC61157
2.142 TEC61157	**0.586** TEC61157	**12.345** TEC61157

Perimeter Cards

Use with "Find Five Pairs" on page 7.

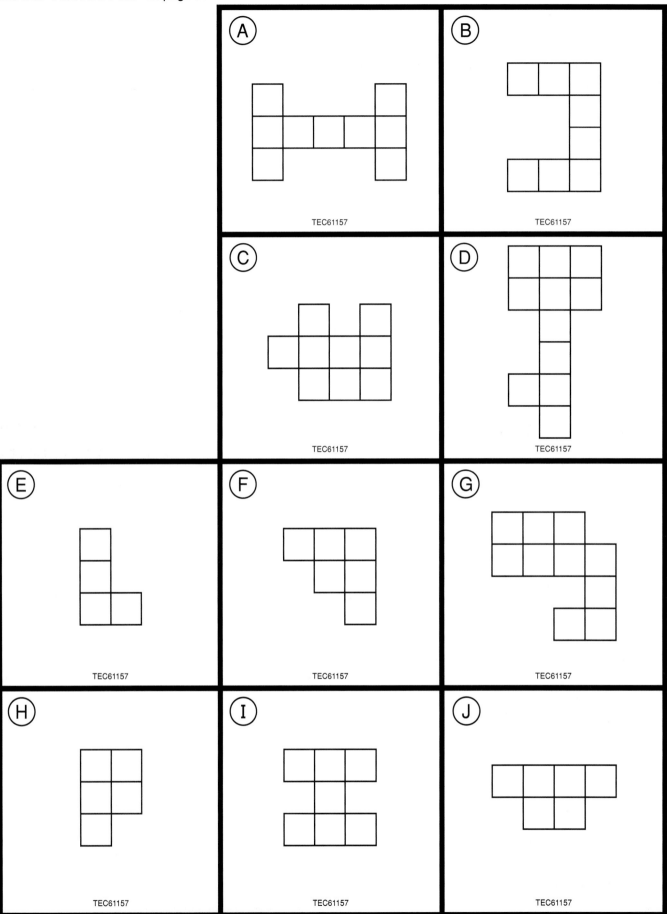

Sandwich Shack

Sandwich	Calories	Sandwich	Calories
Bossy Aussie	260	Gold Rigger	560
Burrito Bandito	490	Ham Slammer	530
Cheddar Shredder	420	Happy Pappy	330
Crusty Musty	270	Shopper Stopper	530
Feast Beast	870	Snack Stack	550
Fish Squisher	730	Sourdough Sloppy Joe	640

TEC61157

Team Roster

Player	Batting Average
Tank Aaron	0.333
Mickey Bantle	0.313
Frank Bromas	0.285
Tom Clavine	0.188
Wade Cloggs	0.289
Cal Dipken	0.304
Ken Driffey	0.303
Reggie Gackson	0.312
Mike Jiazza	0.297
Joe Klizaggio	0.299
Derek Leter	0.298
Orel Mershiser	0.197
Randy Mohnson	0.205
Greg Naddux	0.215
Willie Nays	0.300
Albert Nujols	0.311
Sammy Rosa	0.310
Robin Sentura	0.291
David Sortiz	0.212
Alex Vodriguez	0.296
Chipper Vones	0.302
Roger Yemens	0.191
John Zoltz	0.276
Andruw Zones	0.306

TEC61157

Measuring to the Nearest...

Object	Customary				Metric	
	Inch	Half Inch	Quarter Inch	Eighth Inch	Centimeter	Millimeter
1.						
2.						
3.						
4.						
5.						
6.						
7.						
8.						
9.						
10.						

Super Simple Independent Practice: Math • ©The Mailbox® Books • TEC61157

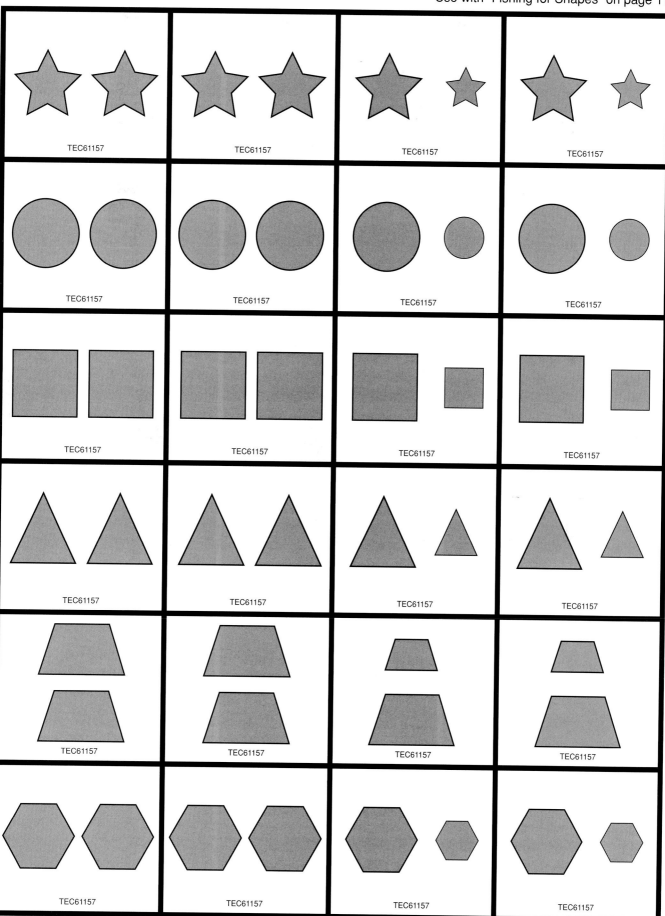

Guest Checks

Use with "Check, Please!" on page 12.

Guest Check

Date	Table Number	Number in Party	Check Number											

TEC61157

Guest Check

Date	Table Number	Number in Party	Check Number											

TEC61157

TEC61157

TEC61157

TEC61157

0.8	800 thousandths	eight tenths	0.800
0.80	eighty hundredths	1.15	one and fifteen hundredths
1.1500	1.150	one and one hundred fifty thousandths	one and fifteen ten thousandths
eight hundredths	three and six tenths	0.008	8.0
80.0	11.5	1.015	0.04
four tenths	4.00	3.06	one and five thousandths

Number Cards

Use with "Luck of the Roll" on page 14 and "Closer to Zero" on page 16.

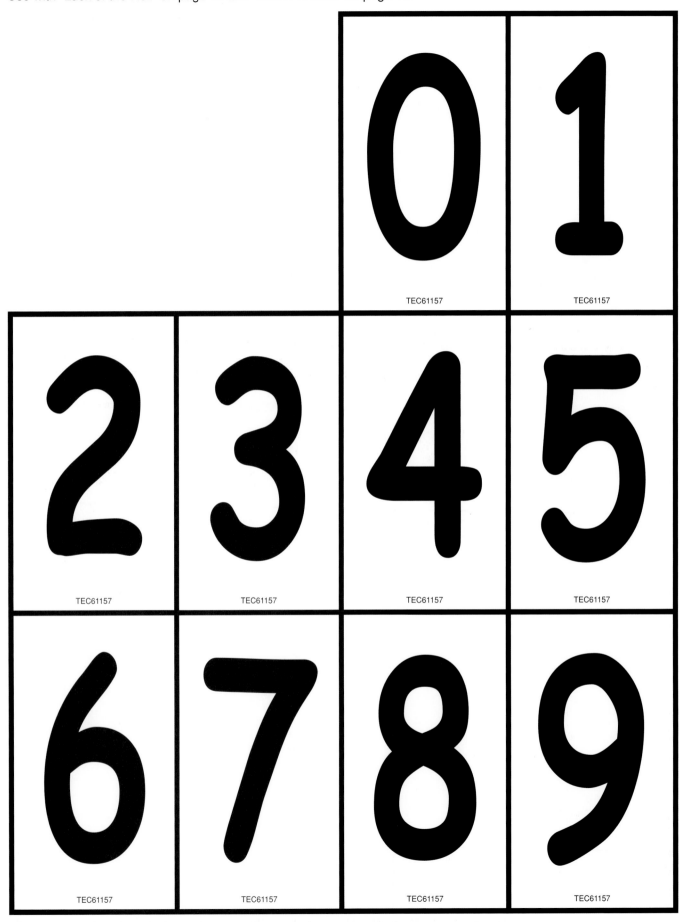

0   1

TEC61157   TEC61157

2   3   4   5

TEC61157   TEC61157   TEC61157   TEC61157

6   7   8   9

TEC61157   TEC61157   TEC61157   TEC61157

Ending Number 10.96 TEC61157	Ending Number 14.93 TEC61157	Ending Number 18.73 TEC61157	Ending Number 13.16 TEC61157	Ending Number 11.56 TEC61157	Ending Number 14.96 TEC61157	Ending Number 9.53 TEC61157	Ending Number 10.16 TEC61157	Ending Number 21.56 TEC61157	Ending Number 30.76 TEC61157
Starting Number 5.6	Starting Number 8.14	Starting Number 11.9	Starting Number 7.8	Starting Number 6.25	Starting Number 9.6	Starting Number 2.7	Starting Number 4.81	Starting Number 16.2	Starting Number 25.44

Name _____   Recording sheet

Go With the Flow!

Starting Number

Add 9.18.

Round the sum to the nearest tenth.

Subtract 2.37 if the nearest tenth of the rounded sum is odd.

Subtract 3.84 if the nearest tenth of the rounded sum is even.

Ending Number

	Card 1	Card 2	Card 3	Card 4	Card 5	Card 6	Card 7	Card 8	Card 9	Card 10

Clue Cards and Answer Key Card

Use with "True or False?" on page 15.

Ⓐ	Ⓑ	Ⓒ
If *s* in this equation represents the length of a square's side, then *p* represents the square's perimeter. $$4s = p$$ TEC61157	This equation shows that y is twice as large as *x*. $$2x = y$$ TEC61157	This expression has more than one correct answer. $$3 + n > 10$$ TEC61157
Ⓓ	Ⓔ	Ⓕ
In this expression, *q* is a positive number less than 35. $$35 - q$$ TEC61157	In this equation, *x* is a variable. $$x + 5 = 14$$ TEC61157	In this equation, *c* is 7. $$8 + c = 14$$ TEC61157
Ⓖ	Ⓗ	Ⓘ
This expression has only one correct answer. $$y - 8 > 2$$ TEC61157	This expression shows that *b* is less than *a*. $$3b < a$$ TEC61157	This number sentence is an equation. $$n - 3 = 10$$ TEC61157

Ⓙ	Answer Key	
This expression means that nine is six more than a number, *x*. $$x - 6 = 9$$ TEC61157	**False**	F G J
	True	A B C D E H I

TEC61157

Super Simple Independent Practice: Math • ©The Mailbox® Books • TEC61157

Math mat

Zigzag Math Path

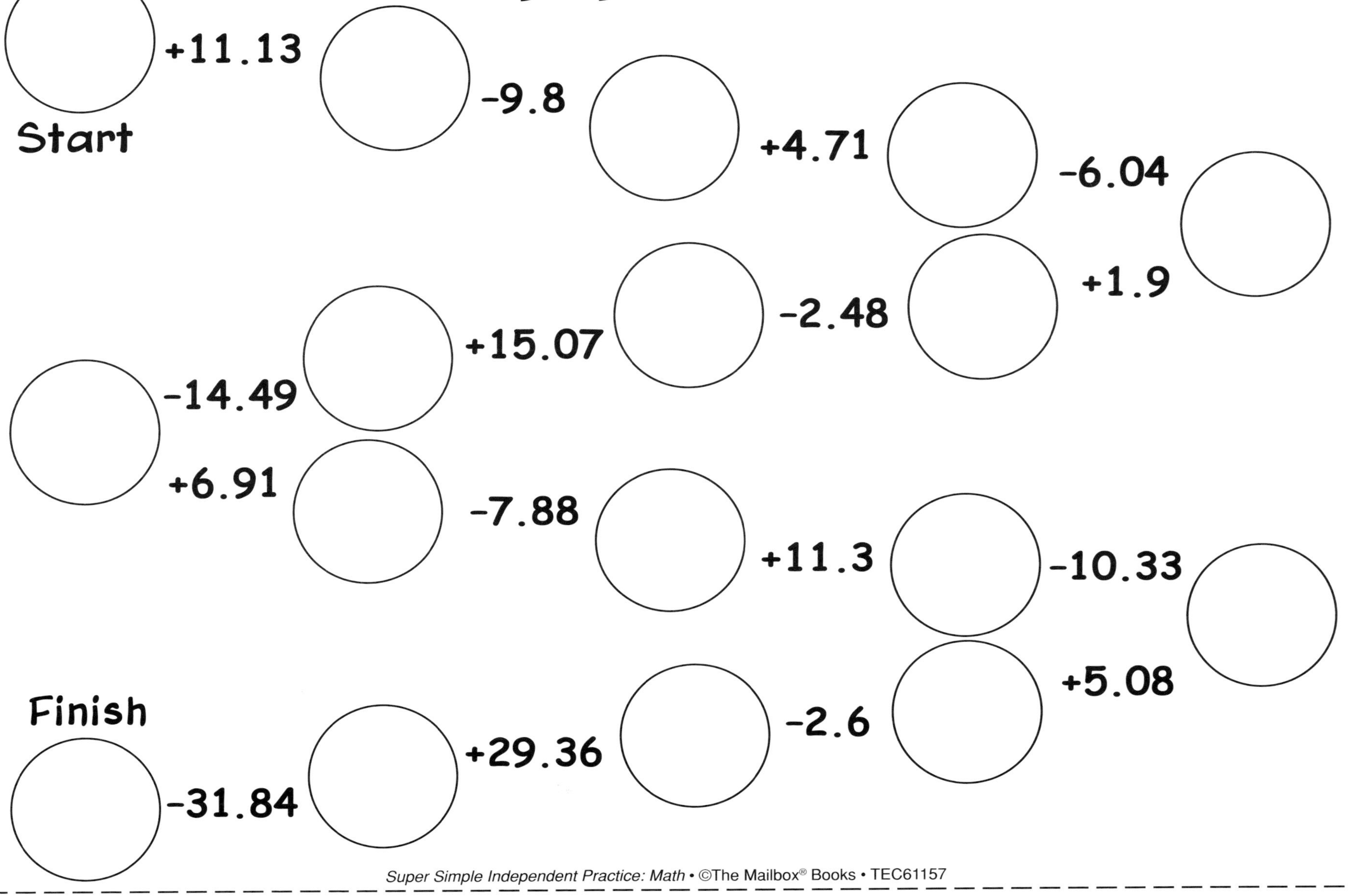

Start

+11.13

−9.8

+4.71

−6.04

−2.48

+1.9

+15.07

−14.49

+6.91

−7.88

+11.3

−10.33

+5.08

+29.36

−2.6

−31.84

Finish

Super Simple Independent Practice: Math • ©The Mailbox® Books • TEC61157

Note to the teacher: Use with "Zigzag Math" on page 20.

Line Segment and Matching Clue Cards

Use with "Measure and Match" on page 21.

Find a segment that is 10 mm long. TEC61157	•——• TEC61157	This segment is 2 mm shorter than 5 cm. TEC61157
•————————• TEC61157	This segment is 55 mm long. TEC61157	(diagonal line segment) TEC61157
(diagonal line segment) TEC61157	Find a segment that is 3.5 cm longer than 10 mm. TEC61157	This segment measures 22 mm. TEC61157
•———• TEC61157	Find a segment that is $\frac{1}{4}$ inch shorter than $1\frac{1}{2}$ inches. TEC61157	•————• TEC61157
This segment measures $1\frac{1}{2}$ inches. TEC61157	•—————• TEC61157	Find a segment that is $\frac{1}{4}$ inch longer than $1\frac{1}{2}$ inches. TEC61157
(diagonal line segment) TEC61157	This segment is $1\frac{7}{8}$ inches long. TEC61157	•——————• TEC61157

Super Simple Independent Practice: Math • ©The Mailbox® Books • TEC61157

Hundred Chart

Use with "Snaking Along" on page 22.

1	2	3	4	5	6	7	8	9	10
11	12	13	14	15	16	17	18	19	20
21	22	23	24	25	26	27	28	29	30
31	32	33	34	35	36	37	38	39	40
41	42	43	44	45	46	47	48	49	50
51	52	53	54	55	56	57	58	59	60
61	62	63	64	65	66	67	68	69	70
71	72	73	74	75	76	77	78	79	80
81	82	83	84	85	86	87	88	89	90
91	92	93	94	95	96	97	98	99	100

TEC61157

Color Problems Chart

Use with "Fishy Products" on page 22.

Color 3

1. $5.25 \times 0.8 = 4.2$
2. $7.5 \times 2.6 = 19.5$
3. $2.45 \times 1.8 = 4.41$
4. $2.16 \times 20 = 43.2$
5. $15.08 \times 2.5 = 37.7$
6. $2.55 \times 8.2 = 20.91$

Color 2

1. $1.75 \times 2.4 = 4.2$
2. $39 \times 0.5 = 19.5$
3. $8.82 \times 0.5 = 4.41$
4. $27 \times 1.6 = 43.2$
5. $7.25 \times 5.2 = 37.7$
6. $5.1 \times 4.1 = 20.91$

TEC61157

Color 1

1. $1.2 \times 3.5 = 4.2$
2. $7.8 \times 2.5 = 19.5$
3. $0.7 \times 6.3 = 4.41$
4. $5.4 \times 8 = 43.2$
5. $5.8 \times 6.5 = 37.7$
6. $6.15 \times 3.4 = 20.91$

Thermometers

Use with "Up and Down the Scale" on page 23.

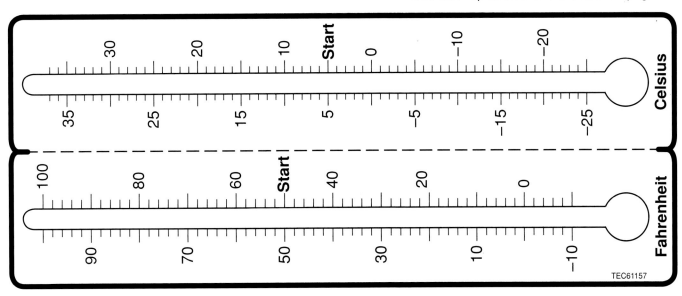

Recording Sheet

Use with "Bottle Cap Dilemma" on page 24.

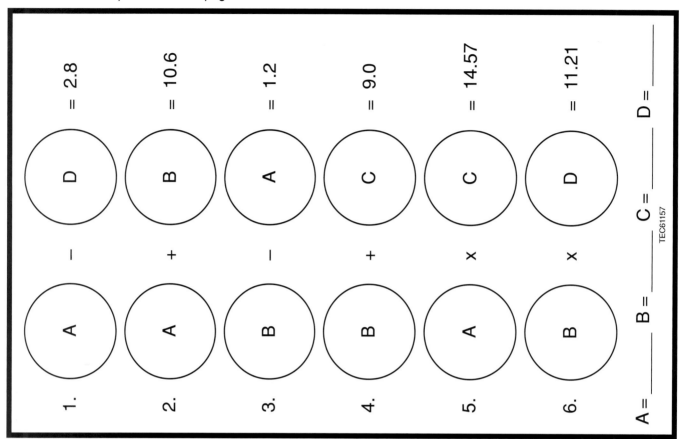

1. $\boxed{A} - \boxed{D} = 2.8$

2. $\boxed{A} + \boxed{B} = 10.6$

3. $\boxed{B} - \boxed{A} = 1.2$

4. $\boxed{B} + \boxed{C} = 9.0$

5. $\boxed{A} \times \boxed{C} = 14.57$

6. $\boxed{B} \times \boxed{D} = 11.21$

A = _____   B = _____   C = _____   D = _____

TEC61157

Number Cards

Use with "Number Trios" on page 26.

9 **29**	
261	
TEC61157	

74 **64**	
4,736	
TEC61157	

71 **592**	
42,032	
TEC61157	

2,744	
49 **56**	
TEC61157	

1,512	
54 **28**	
TEC61157	

4,752	
132 **36**	
TEC61157	

Average Joe's Pizzas

Draw toppings of each kind on the pizzas. Complete the table and chart based on your drawings. Then answer the questions.

Pizza 1
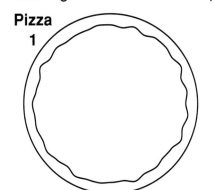

Pizza 2
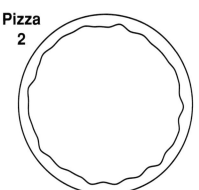

Pizza 3
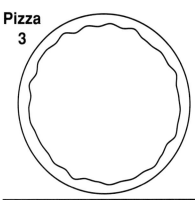

Pizza 4
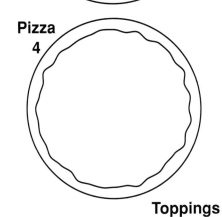

Pizza 5
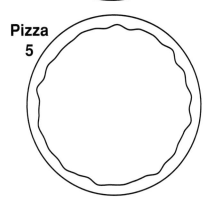

Toppings

yellow	=	onion
red	=	pepperoni
green	=	green pepper
brown	=	mushroom
black	=	anchovy

Toppings

Pizza	Pepperoni	Green Peppers	Mushrooms	Onions	Anchovies
1					
2					
3					
4					
5					
Totals					

Topping	Mean	Median	Mode	Range
pepperoni				
green peppers				
mushrooms				
onions				
anchovies				

Questions	Yes	No
1. Average Joe's Pizzeria promises an average of 11 pepperoni slices per pizza. Is this true?		
2. This store also promises a mean of 15 mushrooms per pizza. Is this true?		
3. At Joe's, the range of pepperoni slices should be less than the range of mushroom slices. Is this true?		
4. Anchovies are expensive, so Joe should use only six anchovies per pizza. Is the mode for anchovies six?		

Super Simple Independent Practice: Math • ©The Mailbox® Books • TEC61157

Daffy Division

Solve.

1. Write the current time on your paper. Rewrite the time as a whole number by replacing the colon with two zeros. For example, 9:26 becomes 90,026. Divide the number by your age.

2. Write the number of letters in each of three sports one after the other. For example, the number of letters in *basketball* (ten), *soccer* (six), and *swimming* (eight) forms 1,068. Divide the number by the number of meals you've eaten at home since Saturday.

3. Write today's date (month/date/year, such as 3/9/08) as a multidigit number (such as 3,908). Divide it by the number of students who are within ten feet of you.

4. Open a textbook and write the page numbers of the two facing pages as one number. Repeat, recording each additional page number as the next digit(s) of the number until it has five to seven digits. Divide it by your shoe size.

5. Write your birthdate as a number. To the right of the last digit, write your favorite number 0–9. Divide the resulting number by the number of windows in the room.

Super Simple Independent Practice: Math • ©The Mailbox® Books • TEC61157

Note to the teacher: Use with "Daffy Division" on page 26.

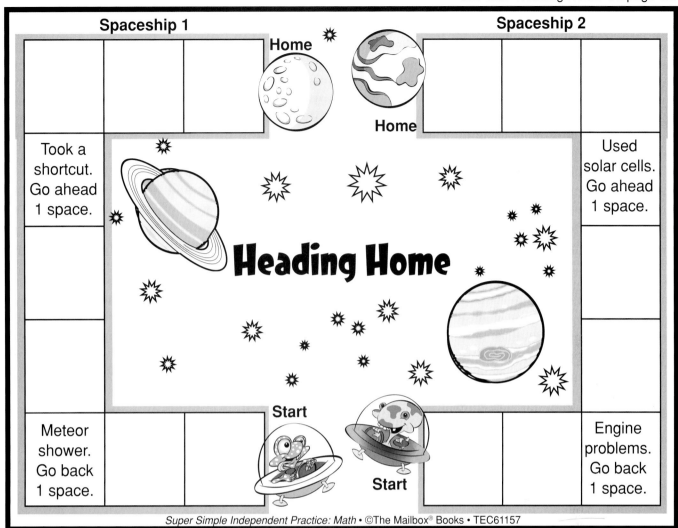

Spaceship 1

Spaceship 2

Home

Home

Took a shortcut. Go ahead 1 space.

Used solar cells. Go ahead 1 space.

Heading Home

Meteor shower. Go back 1 space.

Engine problems. Go back 1 space.

Start

Start

Super Simple Independent Practice: Math • ©The Mailbox® Books • TEC61157

Find Four

$37 + 13 = x$

$60 - x = 10$

What is x? (Your name)

$x \div 2 = 5 \times 5$

$2x - 30 = 70$

$X = 50$

Your name

Steps:

1. Choose any number from 1 to 50.
2. Think of four different expressions whose solution is this number.
3. Write the four expressions and your name on an index card.
4. Write the solution for the expressions and your name on another index card.
5. Put each index card in the correct pocket.

TEC61157

93

Fraction Number Line

Use with "Places, Please!" on page 40.

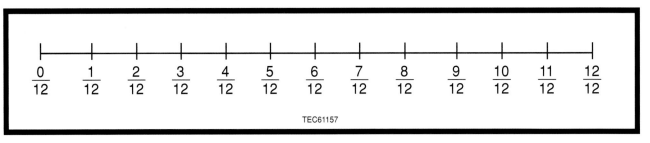

TEC61157

Find the Match!

Read each clue. Look on the thermometer to find the letter of the matching temperature. Cover that letter on your bingo board.

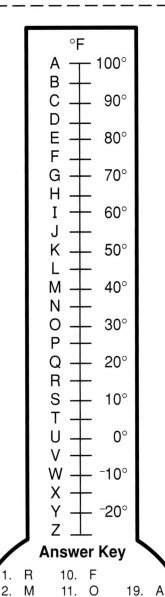

Clues

1. 15° above zero
2. 20° below I
3. 5° warmer than Q
4. 10° cooler than A
5. 15° below zero
6. 5° above zero
7. 20° cooler than J
8. 15° warmer than E
9. 20° cooler than V
10. 30° hotter than L
11. 25° below J
12. 45° above zero
13. 15° below 100°
14. warmer than I, but cooler than 70°
15. cooler than 60°, but warmer than K
16. ⁻5°
17. five degrees warmer than 5°
18. eighty degrees
19. ten degrees warmer than ninety degrees
20. fifty degrees
21. 20° warmer than K
22. fifteen degrees cooler than seventy-five degrees
23. twenty degrees
24. zero degrees
25. ten degrees below zero
26. five degrees warmer than ⁻25°

Answer Key

1. R	10. F		
2. M	11. O	19. A	
3. P	12. L	20. K	
4. C	13. D	21. G	
5. X	14. H	22. I	
6. T	15. J	23. Q	
7. N	16. V	24. U	
8. B	17. S	25. W	
9. Z	18. E	26. Y	

Super Simple Independent Practice: Math • ©The Mailbox® Books • TEC61157

Note to the teacher: Use with "Bingo Solitare" on page 37.

T A S K 1	Construct a figure with an area of 14 square units. Can you construct at least two more?	Possible Solutions for Task 1 TEC61157
T A S K 2	Construct a figure with a perimeter of 12 units. Can you construct two more?	Possible Solutions for Task 2 TEC61157
T A S K 3	Construct a pentagon with an area of five square units.	Solution for Task 3 TEC61157
T A S K 4	Construct a parallelogram with an area of three square units.	Solution for Task 4 TEC61157
T A S K 5	Construct a square whose perimeter is twice its area.	Solution for Task 5 TEC61157
T A S K 6	Construct a square whose perimeter and area are the same.	Solution for Task 6 TEC61157

Puzzle Pieces

Use with "Puzzle Solver" on page 44.

$\frac{24}{27}$ $\frac{9}{21}$	$\frac{8}{9}$ $\frac{6}{7}$ $\frac{10}{12}$	$\frac{24}{28}$ $\frac{3}{48}$ $\frac{6}{8}$	$\frac{1}{16}$ $\frac{12}{15}$
$\frac{3}{7}$ $\frac{15}{27}$ $\frac{4}{36}$	$\frac{5}{6}$ $\frac{5}{9}$ $\frac{3}{10}$ $\frac{2}{16}$	$\frac{3}{4}$ $\frac{6}{20}$ $\frac{1}{8}$ $\frac{2}{6}$	$\frac{4}{5}$ $\frac{3}{24}$ $\frac{3}{21}$
$\frac{1}{9}$ $\frac{2}{24}$ $\frac{6}{10}$	$\frac{1}{8}$ $\frac{1}{12}$ $\frac{21}{27}$ $\frac{3}{18}$	$\frac{1}{3}$ $\frac{7}{9}$ $\frac{4}{7}$ $\frac{1}{3}$	$\frac{1}{7}$ $\frac{8}{14}$ $\frac{2}{10}$
$\frac{3}{5}$ $\frac{5}{9}$	$\frac{1}{6}$ $\frac{10}{18}$ $\frac{21}{30}$	$\frac{5}{15}$ $\frac{7}{10}$ $\frac{10}{14}$	$\frac{1}{5}$ $\frac{5}{7}$

Treasure Chest and Key Patterns

Use with "Code Breakers" on page 45.

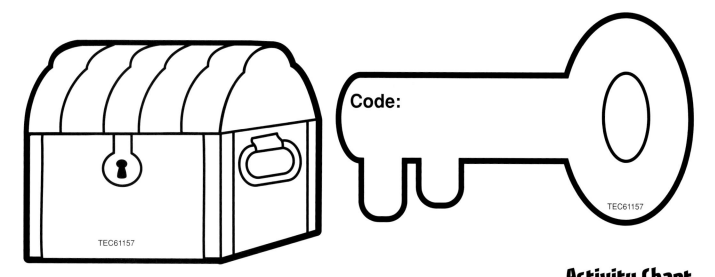

Code:

TEC61157

TEC61157

Activity Chart

Use with "Check the Schedule" on page 45.

Activity	Day	Time
swim team practice	Monday–Friday	7:00 PM–8:00 PM
soccer game	Saturday	9:30 AM–10:30 AM
soccer practice	Monday–Friday	5:30 PM–6:00 PM
tennis lesson	Saturday and Sunday	6:00 PM–6:30 PM
hiking club	Saturday	1:00 PM–6:00 PM
bowling team	Tuesday and Thursday	8:00 PM–9:00 PM

Tree Patterns

Use with "'Tree-mendous'" on page 46.

TEC61157

TEC61157

TEC61157

Cube Pattern

Use with "Picture-Perfect" on page 47, "Roll With It!" on page 58, "Net Worth" on page 65, "On a Roll!" on page 68, "All Decked Out" on page 70, and "Fill'er Up!" on page 71.

Directions for assembling the cube:

1. Cut out the pattern along the solid lines.
2. Fold along the dotted lines.
3. Tape the sides together at the tabs.

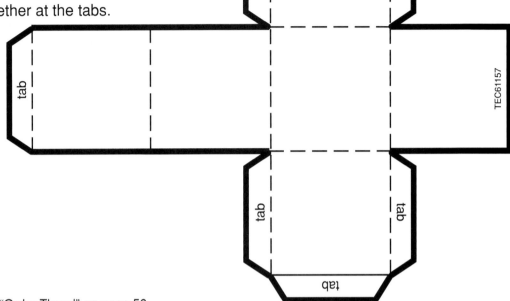

Fraction Strips

Use with "Sweet Treat" and "Order Them!" on page 50.

1											
$\frac{1}{2}$						$\frac{1}{2}$					
$\frac{1}{3}$				$\frac{1}{3}$				$\frac{1}{3}$			
$\frac{1}{4}$			$\frac{1}{4}$			$\frac{1}{4}$			$\frac{1}{4}$		
$\frac{1}{5}$		$\frac{1}{5}$		$\frac{1}{5}$		$\frac{1}{5}$		$\frac{1}{5}$			
$\frac{1}{6}$		$\frac{1}{6}$		$\frac{1}{6}$		$\frac{1}{6}$		$\frac{1}{6}$		$\frac{1}{6}$	
$\frac{1}{7}$	$\frac{1}{7}$		$\frac{1}{7}$		$\frac{1}{7}$		$\frac{1}{7}$		$\frac{1}{7}$		$\frac{1}{7}$
$\frac{1}{8}$	$\frac{1}{8}$	$\frac{1}{8}$		$\frac{1}{8}$		$\frac{1}{8}$		$\frac{1}{8}$		$\frac{1}{8}$	$\frac{1}{8}$
$\frac{1}{9}$	$\frac{1}{9}$	$\frac{1}{9}$	$\frac{1}{9}$		$\frac{1}{9}$		$\frac{1}{9}$	$\frac{1}{9}$		$\frac{1}{9}$	$\frac{1}{9}$
$\frac{1}{10}$	$\frac{1}{10}$	$\frac{1}{10}$	$\frac{1}{10}$	$\frac{1}{10}$		$\frac{1}{10}$	$\frac{1}{10}$	$\frac{1}{10}$	$\frac{1}{10}$	$\frac{1}{10}$	$\frac{1}{10}$
$\frac{1}{11}$	$\frac{1}{11}$	$\frac{1}{11}$	$\frac{1}{11}$	$\frac{1}{11}$	$\frac{1}{11}$	$\frac{1}{11}$	$\frac{1}{11}$	$\frac{1}{11}$	$\frac{1}{11}$	$\frac{1}{11}$	
$\frac{1}{12}$	$\frac{1}{12}$	$\frac{1}{12}$	$\frac{1}{12}$	$\frac{1}{12}$	$\frac{1}{12}$	$\frac{1}{12}$	$\frac{1}{12}$	$\frac{1}{12}$	$\frac{1}{12}$	$\frac{1}{12}$	$\frac{1}{12}$

① half of *b* equals *x* TEC61157	**Ⓔ** ½ *b* = *x* TEC61157	**②** 43 less than *x* equals *y* TEC61157	**Ⓒ** *x* − 43 = *y* TEC61157
③ *x* less than 43 equals *y* TEC61157	**Ⓐ** 43 − *x* = *y* TEC61157	**④** 20 more than *b* TEC61157	**Ⓚ** *b* + 20 TEC61157
⑤ *w* less than 97 TEC61157	**Ⓓ** 97 − *w* TEC61157	**⑥** 12 more than *f* TEC61157	**Ⓑ** *f* + 12 TEC61157
⑦ 2.5 more than *c* TEC61157	**Ⓕ** *c* + 2.5 TEC61157	**⑧** 7 more than *x* equals 21 TEC61157	**Ⓙ** *x* + 7 = 21 TEC61157
⑨ 16 divided by *y* equals *z* TEC61157	**Ⓖ** 16 ÷ *y* = *z* TEC61157	**⑩** 11 times *a* equals *b* TEC61157	**Ⓗ** 11*a* = *b* TEC61157
⑪ 15 less than *e* equals *d* TEC61157	**Ⓘ** *e* − 15 = *d* TEC61157	**Answer Key for "It's a Match!"** 1. E 4. K 7. F 10. H 2. C 5. D 8. J 11. I 3. A 6. B 9. G TEC61157	

Single Quadrant Grid

Use with "Order Up!" on page 56.

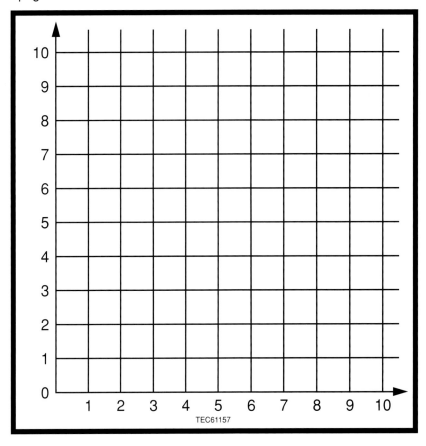

TEC61157

Elapsed time _____

Day of Your Dreams

Activity	Start	Stop	Total Time

Super Simple Independent Practice: Math • ©The Mailbox® Books • TEC61157

Note to the teacher: Use with "Day of Your Dreams" on page 57.

Presidential Birthday Chart

President	Birthday	Birthday as Fraction	President	Birthday	Birthday as Fraction
George Washington	February 22		Grover Cleveland	March 18	
John Adams	October 30		Benjamin Harrison	August 20	
Thomas Jefferson	April 13		William McKinley	January 29	
James Madison	March 16		Theodore Roosevelt	October 27	
James Monroe	April 28		William H. Taft	September 15	
John Q. Adams	July 11		Woodrow Wilson	December 28	
Andrew Jackson	March 15		Warren G. Harding	November 2	
Martin Van Buren	December 5		Calvin Coolidge	July 4	
William H. Harrison	February 9		Herbert C. Hoover	August 10	
John Tyler	March 29		Franklin D. Roosevelt	January 30	
James K. Polk	November 2		Harry S. Truman	May 8	
Zachary Taylor	November 24		Dwight D. Eisenhower	October 14	
Millard Fillmore	January 7		John F. Kennedy	May 29	
Franklin Pierce	November 23		Lyndon B. Johnson	August 27	
James Buchanan	April 23		Richard M. Nixon	January 9	
Abraham Lincoln	February 12		Gerald R. Ford	July 14	
Andrew Johnson	December 29		James E. Carter Jr.	October 1	
Ulysses S. Grant	April 27		Ronald W. Reagan	February 6	
Rutherford B. Hayes	October 4		George H. W. Bush	June 12	
James A. Garfield	November 19		William J. Clinton	August 19	
Chester A. Arthur	October 5		George W. Bush	July 6	

Note to the teacher: Use with "Presidential Birthdays" on page 60.

Flower and Flower Petal Patterns

Use with "Flower Power" on page 60.

TEC61157

TEC61157

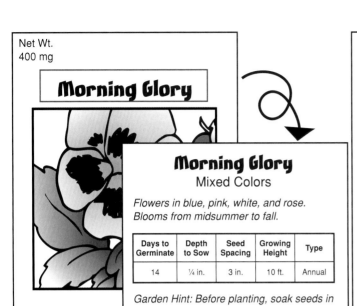

Net Wt.
400 mg

Morning Glory

Morning Glory
Mixed Colors

Flowers in blue, pink, white, and rose. Blooms from midsummer to fall.

Days to Germinate	Depth to Sow	Seed Spacing	Growing Height	Type
14	¼ in.	3 in.	10 ft.	Annual

Garden Hint: Before planting, soak seeds in warm water for 24 hours.

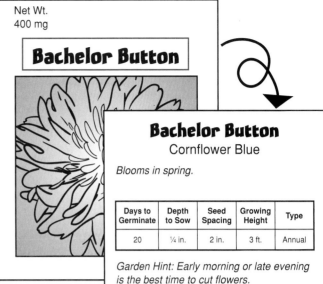

Net Wt.
400 mg

Bachelor Button

Bachelor Button
Cornflower Blue

Blooms in spring.

Days to Germinate	Depth to Sow	Seed Spacing	Growing Height	Type
20	¼ in.	2 in.	3 ft.	Annual

Garden Hint: Early morning or late evening is the best time to cut flowers.

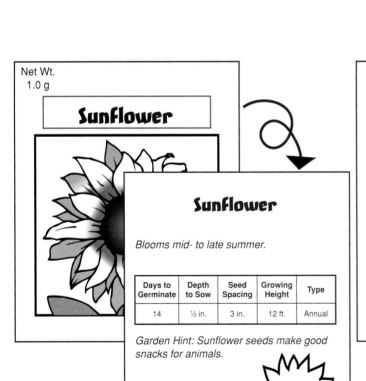

Net Wt.
1.0 g

Sunflower

Sunflower

Blooms mid- to late summer.

Days to Germinate	Depth to Sow	Seed Spacing	Growing Height	Type
14	½ in.	3 in.	12 ft.	Annual

Garden Hint: Sunflower seeds make good snacks for animals.

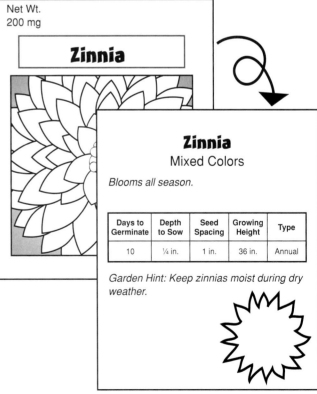

Net Wt.
200 mg

Zinnia

Zinnia
Mixed Colors

Blooms all season.

Days to Germinate	Depth to Sow	Seed Spacing	Growing Height	Type
10	¼ in.	1 in.	36 in.	Annual

Garden Hint: Keep zinnias moist during dry weather.

Super Simple Independent Practice: Math • ©The Mailbox® Books • TEC61157

Note to the teacher: Use with "Planting Time" on page 62.

103

Double Chocolate Cookies

3 c. all-purpose flour
1 tsp. baking soda
$\frac{1}{2}$ tsp. salt
1 c. melted butter
$\frac{3}{4}$ c. white sugar
$\frac{3}{4}$ c. packed brown sugar

1 tsp. vanilla
2 large eggs, beaten
$1\frac{1}{2}$ c. semisweet chocolate chips
1 c. white chocolate chips
$\frac{1}{2}$ c. chopped pecans (optional)

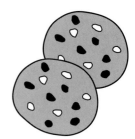

Preheat the oven to 375°. In a small bowl, mix the flour, baking soda, and salt. In a large bowl, beat the butter, white sugar, brown sugar, vanilla, and eggs. Slowly blend the flour mixture into the batter. Stir in the chocolate chips and nuts. Drop spoonfuls of dough about two inches apart onto an ungreased cookie sheet. Bake for 13 to 15 minutes.

Yields 50 cookies.

Double Chocolate Cookies

_____ c. all-purpose flour
_____ tsp. baking soda
_____ tsp. salt
_____ c. melted butter
_____ c. white sugar
_____ c. packed brown sugar

_____ tsp. vanilla
_____ large eggs, beaten
_____ c. semisweet chocolate chips
_____ c. white chocolate chips
_____ c. chopped pecans (optional)

Preheat the oven to 375°. In a small bowl, mix the flour, baking soda, and salt. In a large bowl, beat the butter, white sugar, brown sugar, vanilla, and eggs. Slowly blend the flour mixture into the batter. Stir in the chocolate chips and nuts. Drop spoonfuls of dough about two inches apart onto an ungreased cookie sheet. Bake for 13 to 15 minutes.

Yields _____ cookies.

Super Simple Independent Practice: Math • ©The Mailbox® Books • TEC61157

104 **Note to the teacher:** Use with "Recipe Revisions" on page 64.

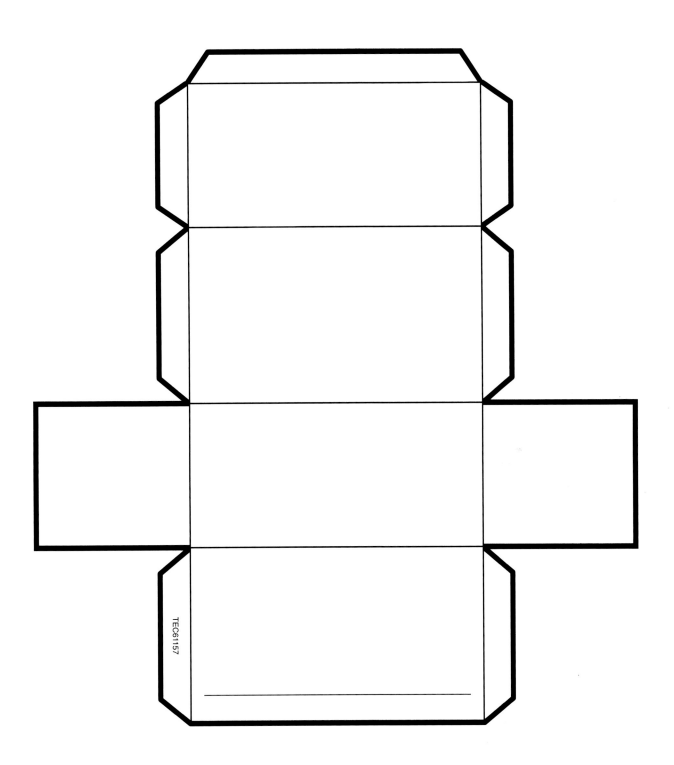

TEC61157

Net Patterns
Use with "Net Worth" on page 65.

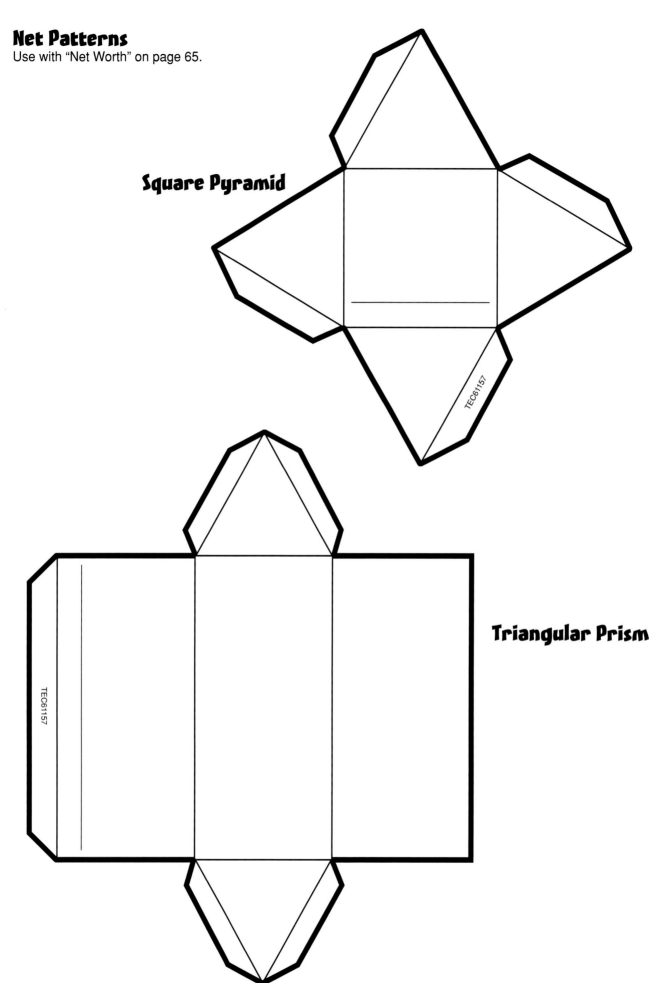

Square Pyramid

TEC61157

Triangular Prism

TEC61157

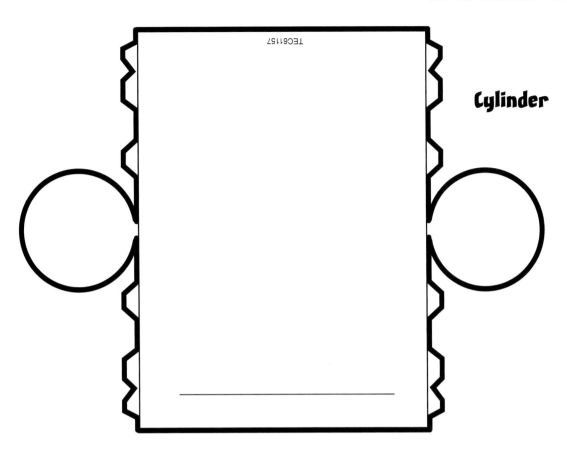

Cylinder

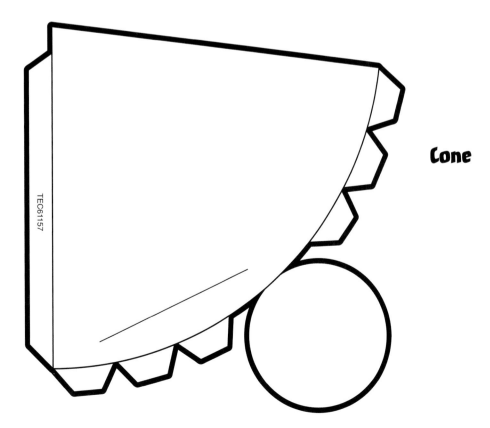

Cone

It's in the Bag!

1. 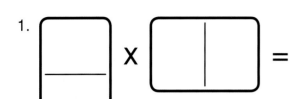 X [|] =

2. [ ] X [|] =

3. [ ] X [|] =

4. [ ] X [|] =

5. [ ] X [|] =

6. 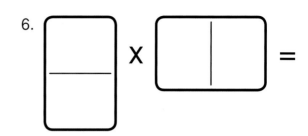 X [|] =

7. 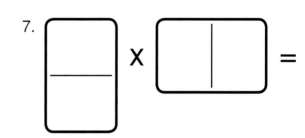 X [|] =

8. [ ] X [|] =

9. [ ] X [|] =

10. [ ] X [|] =

Super Simple Independent Practice: Math • ©The Mailbox® Books • TEC61157

108 **Note to the teacher:** Use with "It's in the Bag!" on page 66.

Bottle Tops

Gameboard A

X	$\frac{1}{2}$	$\frac{2}{3}$	◯
$\frac{4}{5}$	◯	◯	◯
◯	$\frac{1}{4}$	◯	◯
$\frac{1}{4}$	◯	◯	$\frac{1}{12}$

Answer Bank

$\frac{1}{3}$ $\frac{1}{2}$ $\frac{1}{3}$

$\frac{1}{6}$ $\frac{1}{8}$ $\frac{1}{6}$

$\frac{2}{5}$ $\frac{4}{15}$ $\frac{8}{15}$

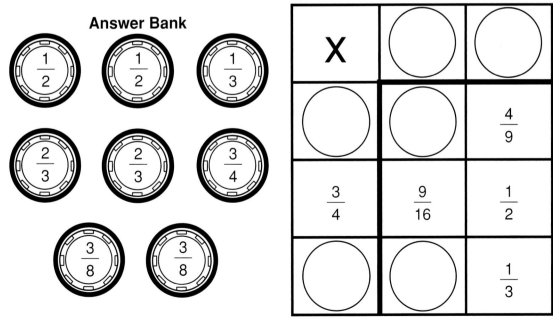

Gameboard B

Answer Bank

$\frac{1}{2}$ $\frac{1}{2}$ $\frac{1}{3}$

$\frac{2}{3}$ $\frac{2}{3}$ $\frac{3}{4}$

$\frac{3}{8}$ $\frac{3}{8}$

X	◯	◯	$\frac{1}{2}$
◯	◯	$\frac{4}{9}$	◯
$\frac{3}{4}$	$\frac{9}{16}$	$\frac{1}{2}$	◯
◯	◯	$\frac{1}{3}$	$\frac{1}{4}$

Note to the teacher: Use with "Bottle Tops" on page 68.

10 x 10 Grid

Use with "Graphic Math" on page 72.

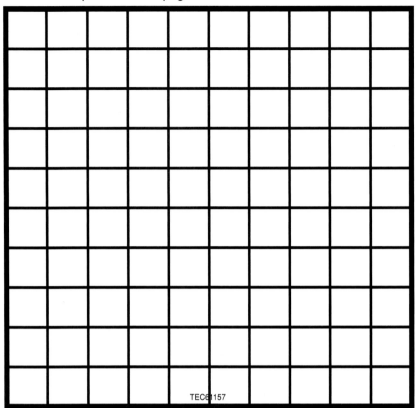

TEC61157

Input-Output Tables

Use with "What's the Rule?" on page 75.

Input	Output
0	8
1	
	13
9	
Rule:	

Input	Output
	$11\frac{1}{2}$
24	
29	$23\frac{1}{2}$
	$59\frac{1}{2}$
Rule:	

Input	Output
	36
10.5	
	27
10	20
Rule:	

Input	Output
	2
	50
	8
100	10
Rule:	

TEC61157

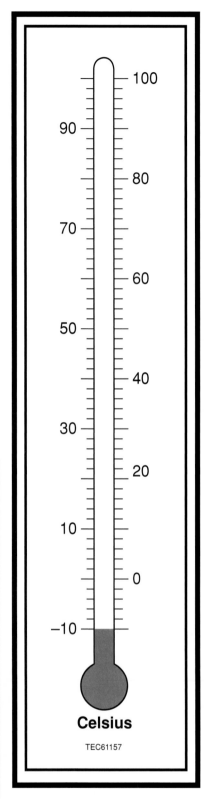

Celsius

TEC61157

Super Simple Independent Practice: Math • ©The Mailbox® Books • TEC61157

Skills Index

Problem Solving